# KUNDALINI:

# AN INDIAN PARADIGM

# OF

# CREATIVITY

By

## Maj Gen. GD Bakshi, SM, VSM

**PILGRIMS PUBLISHING**
◆ Varanasi ◆

**KUNDALINI:** AN INDIAN PARADIGM OF CREATIVITY
Mag. Gen. GD Bakshi, SM, VSM

*Published by:*
PILGRIMS PUBLISHING

*An imprint of:*
PILGRIMS BOOK HOUSE
*(Distributors in India)*
B 27/98 A-8, Nawabganj Road
Durga Kund, Varanasi-221010, India
Tel: 91-542- 2314060  Fax: 91-542-2312456
E-mail: pilgrims@satyam.net.in
Website: www.pilgrimsbooks.com

PILGRIMS BOOK HOUSE (New Delhi)
9 Netaji Subhash Marg, 2nd Floor
Daryaganj, New Delhi 110002
Tel: 91-11-23285081
E-mail: pilgrim@del2.vsnl.net.in

*Edited by* Christopher N Burchett
*Layout & Cover design by* Asha Mishra

ISBN: 81-7769-212-7

*Printed in India at Pilgrim Press Pvt. Ltd. Lalpur Varanasi*

**Dedicated
To
my great teacher
Swami Pranvananda Saraswati
an Engineer
who renounced life to become
a sage in a deep forest.
This book is based on his teachings and
experiences.**

*Gurur Brahma, Guru Vishnu, Guru Devo Maheshwara,
Guru Sakshat Para Brahma, Tasmai Shri Guruve Namaha*

# TABLE OF CONTENTS

# PROLOGUE

# CREATIVITY: THE KUNDALINI PARADIGM

## The Symbols of Creativity

Creativity is the key resource that is responsible for the progress of human civilisation. Physiological creativity is responsible for the propagation of the species. Artistic, intellectual and scientific creativity is the key to the rise of human civilisation and all progress. The cultures of the East, in specific the Indian Civilisation, had worshipped this creative faculty in man. In Indian philosophy it is variously expressed as the Kundalini, the mythical, latent "Serpent" energy whose release leads to the unfolding of a brilliant, creative intelligence in man. It also supposedly enhances individual charisma and communication abilities. The full release of this creative potential confers the mythical Nirvana or liberation experience. Liberation from our existing worldview and paradigms; our conditioned acceptance of the Space-Time that we perceive around us and final merging of the individual consciousness in the transpersonal cosmic consciousness. The release of these latent human potentials acts upon the observer himself and so creates a revolution in his perception of external reality. What exactly is this Kundalini that has so dominated Indian philosophy and mystic thought for centuries? It was my teacher's contention that this Kundalini motif is a subconscious symbol. An insight thrown up by the unconscious mind which in pictorial terms seek to express deep abstract truths. This discovery had laid the foundations of Organic Chemistry. Kekule had been working for a long time to unravel the structure of the Benzene molecule. One day he had a vivid dream in which he saw two snakes, each biting the other's tail in a ring like formation. In a flash of insight he understood this visual cue from his subconscious mind. It helped him to identify the ring structure of the Benzene molecule. This example is often cited as a classic example of dynamic creativity.

The Kundalini symbol of the mythical, reptilian energy coiled up at the base of the spine could well be such an imagic insight which has to be interpreted correctly in the light of recent scientific discoveries. Possibly the symbol of two snakes coiled up around one another represents the double helix structure of the DNA molecule. It thereby points out to the Kundalini possibly representing latent genetic potentials in the human organism, which could lead to its further evolution in terms of the unfolding of intelligence, of synthesis, of creativity, of charisma and communication skills. Such an individual evolution leads to the growth or revival of a civilisation *per se*. The serpent symbolism is significant. Recent research indicates that the bulk of the Kundalini process can be attributed to the ancient, reptilian structures of the human brain in specific to the Hypothalamus-Pituitary combine and the Limbic system and the Reticular formation in the brain stem. These form the Reptilian core of the human brain. The cortex is a later mammalian acquisition.

Like Kekule's dream insight, the Kundalini motif needs to be reinterpreted in the light of recent discoveries in the field of neurophysiology. It can lead us to some startling speculation and conclusions. The Kundalini phenomenon offers a radically new paradigm of human creativity. This book seeks to define that new paradigm of creativity. Indian philosophy throws up a number of such imagic or unconscious insights, which provide dynamic clues for the understanding of human creativity. Possibly these were the products of the deep reflections of the Indian sages upon these issues. Like Kekule's dream symbol of snakes we cannot take them too literally. We have to reinterpret them in the light of the tremendous leaps we have made in scientific knowledge since those ancient times.

## The Primal Symbols of Creativity

In this book I have concentrated upon five such symbolic insights from Indian philosophy that deal with the nature of the human intelligence and creativity. These imagic insights are: —

**\*The Serpent Energy of the Kundalini:** A Tantric symbolism that possibly depicts the latent genetic potential of the human species. Their release supposedly unleashes ecstasy, super intelligence, coherence, creativity and charisma, the hallmarks of an evolved consciousness. As stated earlier, the serpent symbolism is a clue that indicates the physiological basis of this phenomena and is localised in the Reptilian core of the human brain.

**\*Kala Agni**: The Vedas make no mention of the Kundalini. Instead one finds references to "Kala Agni", the "fire" or the energy of time. Agni and Soma form a dynamic duality in the Vedas. Kala Agni rises. It ascends. As a consequence, a rain of Soma is unleashed and descends upon our consciousness as ecstasy. Kala Agni—the energy of time rises. The arrow of time is reversed. Instead of flowing from the past, into the present and on to the future, the future steps back quantum mechanically to guide the unfolding of the present. This entrains the descent of Soma upon our neurons. The reversal of the arrow of time is a very significant Indian concept that merits greater study and scrutiny and is one of the main themes of this book.

**\*Soma**: The Vedic conception of a psychotropic plant that induced ecstasy and tremendous enhancement of creative abilities. It also acted as a mood elevator that removed the normal withdrawal response from pain and thereby induced fearlessness, grandiosity and euphoria. It was ingested alike by the ancient Aryan kings warriors, and priests to enhance their creative potentials and fighting abilities. Soma was historically the great psychotropic spur to enhancing human creativity to supernal heights. In more scientific terms the upsurge of Soma seems to stem from a release of endorphins and enkephalins in our reptilian brain structure. These opiates of the brain induce ecstasy, mood elevation, euphoria and confer a great rise in the levels of creativity.

**\*The Savitur or the Sun**: The Vedic conception of the Savitur is possibly the most perfect symbol of creativity and synthesis. The blazing sun symbolises the blazing light of super human intelligence. Hydrogen atoms fuse into Helium in the core of the sun. Ideas and concepts fuse in the creative mind to form new insights and discoveries, to seek new and novel relationships between existing ideas.

**\*The Kalpavriksha or the Mythical Wishing Tree**: In symbolic terms the mythical wishing Tree, with roots above and branches below, possibly represents the 'Tree Architecture' of the human mind. The axons and dendrites in the brain are "tree like" in shape. So is the nervous system root like in appearance. If we view the human mind as a bio-computer, it is obvious that its structure is not in the serial or parallel processing mode. Obviously, nature overcame the "Paul Von Neuman bottleneck" in bio-computer architecture aeons ago. The human brain and nervous systems are possibly designed on a Tree architecture. Hence the imagic insight of the mythical wish fulfilling tree which appears even in the early Shamanic lore and later as the Kalpavriksha—the tree that lives for an age.

*Atharvanic Concepts of the Kundalini: Incidentally all these latter four symbols are the key *leit motifs* of the Atharva Veda. The Atharva Veda is the last of the four Vedas and supposedly the most mystical and magical of them all. It is supposed to deal with the "Brahma-Vidya" or the "Science of consciousness". As recent advances in Physics and Quantum mechanics tell us, the observing consciousness cannot be left out of the ambit of our scientific observations and measurements (Hisenberg's Principle). The Vedas do not mention the Kundalini per se. The Vedas however refer to it in the four symbolical terms of the Kala Agni, Soma, the Savitur and the mythical Kalpavriksha (The Tree with Roots above and branches below) that represents the complex architecture of the human bio-computer and the human mind. The earlier Vedas showed an even deeper insight into the Kundalini phenomena that was later the core principle of Tantras. These three symbols (The Soma, the Sun and the Mythical Tree) constitute the core imagic motifs of the Atharva Veda.

## Interpretations of the Imagic Motifs

The Kala Agni, Soma, Savitur and the Kundalini possibly represent processes that bring about the onset of an evolutionary mode of human consciousness. A mode characterised by the predominance of the Right as opposed to the left Brain lobe activity; by the massive release of neuro-peptides in the human brain and Immune System which generate ecstasy, euphoria and mood elevation and acts as a tremendous spur to creativity, learning and longevity.

### Kala Agni: The Vedic concept of the Kundalini

Deep reflection upon these imagic insights from the Atharva Veda, served to highlight a revolutionary new interpretation of the Kundalini process, a Vedic interpretation of the Kundalini as the

Kala Agni. The Vedas do not speak of the Kundalini. They mention instead the "Kala Agni", the energy of time. This is dormant in us. It is kinetised. It rises. Its ascent causes a revolution in our psyche. The direction of the arrow of time is reversed dramatically. The biological organism now is no longer propelled or pushed forward by its evolutionary inheritance of the past (by the past mutation of its genes). Rather it becomes a prophetic life form. It is now *pulled by the future evolutionary potentials*. In terms of the theory of morphic resonance enunciated by Rupert Sheldrake, the future probabilities step back quantum mechanically to guide the growth of the biological organism in the present. This reversal of the arrow of time causes a revolutionary quantum jump in our consciousness. It reaches out to the next level of development.

The Kala Agni goes up, it ascends and the rain of Soma comes down upon our neurons in quantas of polypeptides (Endorphins and Enkephalins of ecstasy and euphoria). Agni rises; Soma descends. Here we have a synthesis of the classical Kundalini of the Tantras with the super mind of Sri Aurobindo.

## Experiential Basis

The venerable Pandit Gopi Krishna did yeomen service by documenting his experiences of the Kundalini in a clinical and objective way. I was set on the same road some twenty-five years ago by my teacher and guide who taught me the practical techniques of meditation. Under his guidance I had some vivid inner experiences and was led to reflect deeply on the classical symbols of the Soma and the Savitur, and the Kundalini, the Kala Agni and the Kalpavriksha Tree. The more I have reflected on these ancient imagic insights, the more they have taught me over the years. In this book I have recorded these reflections, which *seek to reinterpret these archetypal symbols in the light of current knowledge in many diverse fields*. In the main, the contents of this book are the teachings of my spiritual guide and teacher, the late Swami Pranvananda Saraswati. He was a brilliant Engineer who left his career to become a sage in an ancient forest shrine. His life style was a perfect synthesis of the ancient and modern. In the main, it was he who exhorted me to seek a synthesis between modern scientific thought and classical religious experience. This book has been inspired by his life and teachings and his grace.

Today there is a crying need for such a synthesis, for such an overview that links these diverse stands of understanding into a unitary whole is a long overdue. As Marowitz has said, today's specialist is concentrating upon splitting, upon knowing more and more about less and less. He has pointed out the need for "Lumpers" *for people who will lump together or integrate and synthesise these diverse strands into a unitary whole.* There is a need to synthesise the New Physics with the Life Sciences. Integration therefore is the need of the hour, integration as opposed to differentiation and specialisation. This needs generalists who can take an overview with the help of ancient mystic insights and attempt such a  grand unification' or synthesis. I do hope and trust that the reflections in this book will prompt minds far richer than mine to engage themselves in this quest for "Wholeness" and the ultimate synthesis of understanding.

## The Harvest of Hormones

Recent discoveries in neuro-physiology have opened a revolutionary new vista into the working of the human mind. A large number of Western Scientists are now convinced that the human brain is hard wired for these mystical experiences of ecstasy and cosmic consciousness (expansion of being). They are engaged in experiments designed to unravel the neurobiology of Nirvana. Neuro-theology is now a popular new buzzword. The Kundalini represents a full actualisation of human potentials. In fact yoga is aimed at such an actualisation of human potential. **It was my teacher's contention that *Yogic methods employed directed attention at the site of the Pineal or Pituitary master gland and the Endocrine glands to reap a harvest of the desired neurotransmitters and Hormones*. The Vedic Seers and Tantric masters were engaged in *this inner agriculture* to reap the harvest of hormones.** The prize jewels of the "Soma" were complex neuro-peptides like the Endorphins and Enkephalins class of opiates generated by the human brain during meditative practices. These lead to ecstasy and mood elevation and play a major role in the alleviation of pain and in the process of learning. The so-called classical "Nirvana" experience was possibly bio-chemically induced by the eruption of these Neuro-peptides in the brain. This inner harvesting will possibly help the human race to realise its full Evolutionary potential. And when man does actualise his full evolutionary potential, human civilisation will scale dizzy new heights of achievement. That is what the future is all about. A quest for synthesis and integration; a grand unified field theory that includes consciousness and the observer in its encompass; a holistic overview that unifies and binds together the *diverse strands of human knowledge and experience.*

This book seeks to present new interpretations of the ancient concept of the Kundalini. In specific it propounds the Vedic concept of the Kundalini as the concerted action of Kala Agni and Soma. The concerted actions of this pair of primal forces brings about our evolution. The Kundalini in essence is the Indian paradigm of creativity.

# CHAPTER ONE

# THIRD WAVE REFLECTIONS ON CREATIVITY

## A Theory of Conflict

The future concerns us all. For whether we like it or not, we are all being driven inexorably towards the future by the relentless tide of time. The poet T.S. Eliot had said, "time past and time present are both present in time future". Predicting that future from models built up from the patterns of the past and present is what Futurology is all about. Alwyn Toffler made the future a household word with his book "Future Shock." With his magnum opus the "Third Wave" he acquired the status of a cult figure—a guru, of the future. His stellar contribution has been to provide us with analytical tools with which we can dissect history, with which we can isolate trends and patterns and build heuristic models that can help us to predict the shape of things to come. His theory of the three waves of history has been an intellectual landmark of sorts and his entire works provide us with a new ideology that seems to transcend national boundaries. It is an ideology woven around the future. Toffler theorised about three waves of civilisation based on three scientific revolutions. These were: —

(a) **The First Wave.** (8000 B.C. to 1600 A.D.) Based upon the Agricultural Revolution.

**(b)  The Second Wave**. (1600 A.D. to 1950 A.D.) Based upon the Industrial Revolution.

**(c)  The Third Wave**. (1950 A.D. onwards.) Based upon the Electronic Revolution.

*The Agricultural revolution, the Industrial revolution and the electronic revolution are the three waves of history.* The central metaphor of Toffler's magnum opus "The Third wave" was a "clash of waves". The second and the third waves are as dissimilar to each other as the first and the second waves were. The clash of the first and second waves saw the upsurge of the western civilisation and the imperial drive that led to colonisation of the First wave cultures of the East. Within second wave societies themselves, the clash of first and second wave ideologies led to violent conflict. The French Revolution, the Russian Revolution, the American Civil War and the Mejjei Restoration in Japan are all representative of this clash of waves, where two dissimilar wave fronts meet, historical interference patterns and dark bands are bound to arise. Toffler's thesis provides us with a new theory of conflict based upon the physics of wave front reconstruction.

**The Harmony of Waves (Third World: Third Wave)**

The central metaphor of this book is a harmony of waves. Toffler himself has pointed out the similarities between the First and Third wave cultures. It is my contention that these two waves are synchronous, they are in step or in phase. This is because essentially both of them are organic cultures. *The central motif of the First wave agricultural society was organic growth. Its energy base was drawn from the sun and the climatic cycles.* The central motif of the second wave however was artificial production. Its energy base lay in the inert fossil fuels. The rapacious way in which industrial society set about destroying our ecosystems, has brought mankind to this serious condition of crisis. Where the First wave relied on the solar energy of fusion and synthesis, the central paradigm of the second wave has been fission, differentiation, specialisation and entropy. The sorry pass to which we have brought ourselves, the acute crisis in the human condition today, underlines the crying need for synthesis and integration. That indeed will be the central motif of the Third wave civilisation. With its reliance on Electronics, Bio-technology and *renewable sources of Energy* it will *return to the core-motif of organic growth as opposed to artificial production: to Fusion as opposed to Fission.* On the philosophical plane it will derive its inspirational inputs from Eastern mysticism and not atomistic Greek thought. This book seeks to identify these inspirational inputs from Eastern mysticism that will go a long way to mould the shape of things to come in the Third Wave civilisation. It goes so far as to *speculate that the Third Wave will occur primarily in the "Third World", in ancient First Wave civilisations not fully corroded by the malaise of industrialism.* Toffler himself had foreseen the end of the "white interlude" in human history. With this end, Eastern philosophies and worldviews will once again come back into fashion. The application of the tenets of Eastern mysticism could well alter our basic paradigms in science. The same has already happened in Physics where quantum mechanical thought sounds more and more like the paradoxical logic of Vedanta or Zen. The other sciences, especially the life sciences, are bound to follow suit. This book *seeks to speculate on these issues.*

## Cultivating the C-3 Resources of Creativity, Charisma and Communication Skills

A progressive analysis of the three waves shows that the *need to foster creativity by promoting greater leisure has been an unconscious guiding principle of evolutionary growth.* The

First Wave civilisation relied on human and animal muscle power. This led the mass of mankind to engage in back breaking labour in the fields. *Guidance was provided by small feudal or creative minorities that were kept in leisure by the toil of the masses.* In the Second Wave, electro-mechanical machines freed human beings of the need for physical toil and labour in the fields. Theoretically it should have generated greater leisure but *in practice it uprooted masses of humanity from the fields and concentrated them in dehumanising industrial slums and ghettos. Work in the industrial environment was cruelly repetitive and mechanical.* There was an incredible increase in the level of information in the industrial society. Just as it was threatening to burst asunder with the weight of this informational overload, came the Third Revolution—the electronic revolution that freed the human neurons of the strain of routine computation and memorisation; even as the Second wave electromechanical machines had freed the human muscles of physical strain. *This has generated greater and greater leisure. Leisure, which is the spur to creativity. Creativity then is a key resource without which no civilisation can ever aspire to greatness.* In ancient India, vast segments of the population retired to the Buddhist monasteries, to the Chaityas and Vihars. This age saw an incredible upsurge in creativity. This has left its indelible impact in the frescoes of Ajanta and the rock cuts caves of Ellora and elsewhere in painting, art, architecture and sculpture. Another vital ingredient for national greatness is *charismatic leadership*. A leadership imbued with the $C^3$ assets of creativity, charisma and phenomenal communication or rhetorical skills to programme the collective conscious of a people is a prerequisite for that civilisation's march to greatness.

How do these $C^3$ assets arise? How are these triple resources of creativity, charisma and communication skills generated? Are they accidental genetic spin-offs; chance products that suddenly provide the impetus for the rise of a civilisation? The rise and fall of civilisations does not appear to rest on such random or chance factors. *Myths and legends prevalent in some Eastern cultures speculate that these human resources could be consciously cultivated.* The Indian concept of the Kundalini possibly represented a *Hindu paradigm of such evolution; an evolution of consciousness that led to an upsurge of these $C^3$ resources in mankind.* The rise of such $C^3$ resources led *to the rise of prophets and Buddhas and Avatars*, men endowed with phenomenal charisma; men who provided the ideological political or military leadership for their race. Religion, after all is an ideology, even as Marxism, Maoism, Nazism or Zionism are ideologies.

## Kundalini: Release of Latent Genetic Potentials

This book is essentially about the Kundalini, the mythical evolutionary faculty inbuilt into the human species. The ancient First Wave civilisation of India worshipped this as the source of all human creativity. What is of significance is the written and oral tradition that prescribed the life styles and psychosomatic exercises *specifically designed to "arouse" or activate this biological mechanism of human evolution.* No man has done greater service to the cause of this ancient tradition than the late Pandit Gopi Krishna, who has left behind a remarkable clinical account of the "activation" of this genetic mechanism in his own being. *This genetic mechanism holds great promise in our study and understanding of the phenomena of creativity and charisma.* These will indeed be the key resources of the Third Wave civilisation that will be based on synthesis. This book then, is a radical reinterpretation of the Kundalini, that ancient Indian concept of creativity; creativity that was, that is and that will ever continue to be the chief resource of any civilisation aspiring for historical greatness.

# CHAPTER TWO

## CREATIVITY, CHARISMA AND COMMUNICATION SKILLS

Evolution is a creative process. Any changes that enhance human creative potentials then, are significant mediators for evolutionary growth of the species. For the maximisation of our creative potentials indeed is the key to hastening our evolutionary processes. That is the way evolution is unfolding itself in the Homo sapiens by successfully enriching the neural circuitry of the human brain. Creative upsurges in mankind represent such a state of growth in the neuron circuitry-each new act of creation-represents the birth of a new neural connection somewhere in some human brain.

There appears to be collective species field in such matters. *Rupert Sheldrake has called it the morphogenetic field. Once a new skill has been learnt by one member of the species— subsequent learning of the same skill by other members all over the planet becomes much faster and easier.* Sheldrake has demonstrated this by empirical experiments conducted on rats. Once one set of rats learnt to run a particular maze, other rats of the species take appreciably less time to acquire the same skill anywhere on the planet. Apparently the inverse square law does not seem to have any bearing upon the transference of these acquired abilities amongst the species. A new neuron circuit actualised in one particular brain represents the birth of a new knowledge circuit. Once it is "born" or actualised its subsequent rebirth or transference to other brains within the same species becomes markedly easier. Only the first creative leap has to overcome the forces of inertia that seem to oppose change. The struggle is involved only in the first attempt that breaches a virgin landscape— that etches a new furrow neural or interconnection. *There appears to be a "hologramic" relationship between each individual brain of the particular species and the overall "morphogenetic field of the species". Each part seems to contain the whole even as every molecule of a hologram contains the whole picture.* Geographical distance or separation of the two brains does not seem to attenuate the strength of the new impulse. It propagates in a universal fashion through the species morphogenetic field that affects all individual species brains all over the planet. In our times we have seen the upsurge of new ideas—the birth of new concepts simultaneously in a number of different minds widely separated by geographical distances. Very often scientists working separately in the erstwhile Soviet Union and the United States or Japan or Europe have simultaneously achieved breakthroughs in the same field of endeavour—without even being aware of the efforts of the others in that field. *Concepts like archetypes descend past the filters and gates of reality. Often they are "born" at the same time in many minds widely separated by geographical distances.* The real nature of the morphogenetic species field, if it exists, and its interrelationships with the individual brains of the species are matters of philosophical conjecture as yet. But they will have a shattering impact on man's understanding of his universe in the times to come.

Scientists like H E. Puthoff, R. Trag, C. E. Tart and others have conducted studies on Anomalous phenomena of consciousness. In specific they have studied, "perceptual channels for information transfer over kilometre distances". Extensive studies and experiments were carried out at the Princeton University and Stanford Research Laboratories in the USA. The CIA was involved in "psychic espionage", using sensitive/gifted individuals for "Remote Viewing" of target sites in the Soviet Union. These experiments have highlighted *the non-local nature of consciousness not only in space but also in time—extending even into the future.*

There are therefore remarkable talents and gifts encoded in the human consciousness, which can extend the envelope of man's Extra Sensory Perception (ESP) far beyond the normal or the known. *Arthur Koestler had coined the word "bisosciation" to explain the basis of human creativity. In his magnum opus "The Act of Creation", he described the creative act as the leap (or the quantum jump) from one universe of discourse to another disparate universe. Creativity is the ability to see inter connections or new relationships between unrelated concepts or thought matrices.* The commonest example of the creative act is humour—the paroxysm of laughter that erupt—when we succeed in establishing the relationship between two diverse strands of meaning in a joke. The triumphant "Ha" that signifies the catharsis or release of emotional energies mobilised to identify the hidden link between two parallel universes of discourse in a simple joke or comic episode, are the commonest examples of creativity. Creativity works everywhere in the same quantum fashion. Archimedes struggles over the problem of identifying the impurity in the king's crown without taking it apart. He is engrossed with this problem. He enters the bathtub and feels himself lighter in the water. In a flash his mind takes the quantum leap from his lightness in the bath to the specific gravity of the crown. The considerable emotional and mental energies mobilised in the problem solving process are now siphoned off in a tremendous "EUREKA"—whoop.

The "Eureka" whoop of triumph celebrates the birth of a brand new neural connection. *Lateral thinking or thinking that con-*

*nects diverse matrices of thought is the mechanism that etches these circuits.* Neural connections are mediated by the processes of abstraction. Bisosciation—the leap from one neural pathway to another is expressed in neuro-physiological terms by the etching of a new circuit that interlinks existing strands of neural chains. As this analysis reveals there is a definite *need to mobilise man's emotional energy potential for etching this new circuitry. There is definite linkage between this mobilisation of emotional energies and creativity.* The cathartic release of laughter, of Bathos or Pathos—of the HA or the AH—the strength of the Eureka whoop clearly points out to *the energetic basis of the process. The emotional sexual fuels that power our instinctual drives seem to be the welding torches that help solder new inter-neuron connections in the human brain.* The welding elements that solder such neuron circuits are provided by the Neuro transmitters, the single amino acids, the monoamines and polypeptides. The human bio-computer is programmed by the language code of these neurotransmitters. One neuron "speaks" to another with the help of these simple Sodium Potassium or Calcium ions— these amino acids the more complex peptides and the far more sophisticated polypeptides. The energy base of the bio-computer is generated by the burning of glucose in the glial cells of the brain. The neuro-transmitters are also the trigger signals that control our moods and emotions and fuel our sexual drives. The same trigger elements are involved in more subtle ways in creative processes of responding to the social and environmental challenges.

## The Calcium—Fodrin-Caplin Cascade: The Soldering Mechanism

Recent researches in neuro-physiology have shown that neuro-peptides seem to play a significant role in the learning process. A possible "soldering" mechanism for etching new neural connections in the brain (which could be the physical agency for "rewiring" to accommodate new memory traces in the brain) has been suggested by Gary Lynch and his colleague Michel Bandry of the University of California. In their experiments on rat brain tissues they stimulated the Hippocampal neurons with electrical pulses. They discovered that the post synoptic cells became inundated with large amounts of calcium ions. These ions in turn activated a dormant enzyme called Caplain. Now Caplain's primary role is to break down certain proteins. Fodrin (a protein) is the major structural component of the spines of neurons. When Caplain begins to break down Fodrin-extra receptors for the neuro-transmitter Glutamate are exposed. This makes the neurons more responsive to Glutamate and they are better able to communicate with one another. When repeatedly stimulated, more Calcium ions enter the cells, causing Caplain to break down more Fodrin. At this point the constant breaking down of Fodrin causes the neuron spine to change its shape and form new spines and ridges. This Calcium—Caplain-Fodrin Cascade has been suggested as the mechanism for recording memory traces or for forming new inter-neural connections. Interpreting Koestler's thesis of Bisosciation— these new inter neural connections perhaps help us to do "lateral thinking", to take the quantum leap from one matrix of thought (as represented by one neural chain) to another.

*An electron can jump to the next orbital or energy level only if it receives a charge of energy. It can stay in that "excited" condition only as long as the energy input lasts. When it falls back to its lower energy state, it gives out a quanta or package of energy equal to the potential difference between the two energy levels.* The same quantum analogy is valid at the ideative level. To take the quantum jump from one matrix of thought to the next requires a charge of neural "energy". *Once the linkage is established between the two matrices, the energy charge becomes redundant and has to be siphoned off in a Eureka whoop, in laughter or even tears.* What is the basis of this "neural energy" in the cores of our brain? Is it produced by the burning of glucose fuels in the glial cells of our brain? Is it the complex of emotional-sexual energies that Freud referred to as the Libido? At the neuro-physiologic level it is expressed as a release of neuro-peptides and neuro-transmitters by the master glands of the endocrine system. At the network level it is expressed in terms of new inter-neuron pathways and connections.

The key to human evolution and growth as a species then is to prompt and stimulate these creative resources and extra sensory perception abilities in mankind. Neuro-physiological evolution proceeds by such enrichment of our neural circuitry. Its external manifestations are expressed in terms of the enrichment of the quality of human civilisation. ORGANIC GROWTH—not struggle—is its key metaphor.

## Charisma

When we speak of the growth of civilisation—we have to turn to the historians to help us analyse and identify these growth patterns. There are two schools of thought amongst historians—the Marxist school of history and the Western or Toynbee's school. The Marxist view lays stress on the Forces of History—as the key elements that mould the destinies of peoples and bring about the rise and fall of civilisations. The Marxist viewpoint was obsessed with the economic aspect of human existence. Marxist philosophers sought to link their philosophy with the biological theory of evolution. Marxism however was a social philosophy relevant only to the age of industrialism. It was a narrow, tunnelised viewpoint for it sought to interpret the alpha and omega of human existence from the economic viewpoint alone. It was therefore, a narrow and "tunnelised" worldview that refused to look beyond the economic blinkers that restricted its field of vision. Economic activity is only one aspect of human life. An obsession with the economic factors may have been reasonable in that period of flux when agricultural societies were being savagely uprooted to erect the edifice of an industrial civilisation. Primitive social hierarchies of feudalism acquired control of the means of production and their untamed greed led them to exploit their work force in a brutal and inhuman manner. Marxist philosophers sought to put the control of the means of production back in the hands of the workers. But it had no qualms against industrialisation and its mechanisation and dehumanisation of society. To that extent Toffler is right in his assumption that *Socialism and Capitalism are both simply two aspects of the same industrial reality.* The social structure of society may be different but both operate well within the framework of the industrial paradigm; the universe of electro-mechanical machines, giant factories and mills and dehumanised assembly lines. In seeking to amplify the power of human musculature, both these arrogant philosophies divorced themselves from the ecological principles of organic growth—to artificial "Production". The simple agricultural cycles and feedback loops were torn apart. The entrails of the earth were gouged open to dip into the dead fossil base of the planet and use these to generate energies to move the engines of the industrial society. *The reliance on dead fossil fuels divorced man from the living sources of energy—from the sunlight and climatic cycle that had fuelled his agriculture. In divorcing himself from these living sources man began to destroy the finely tuned systems that regulated life in this biosphere.* Exaggerated emphasis on one aspect of life can lead to such distorted viewpoints. The industrial civilisation has led to unsustainable growth. It has thoughtlessly dipped into the Earth's capital of carbon fuels. Evolution took billions of years to fix the carbon from the earth's atmospheres to its surface and subsurface as fossil fuels. In just one century man has burnt the bulk of it back into the terrestrial atmosphere. In the next 50 years he is likely to burn back the balance fossil fuels. The earth would soon resemble Venus or Mars. It is likely to breed ecological disaster of a planetary magnitude. Still, the Marxist viewpoint had much to recommend it. It consciously sought to link its philosophical base with the scientific Paradigm of evolution. In the Marxian interpretation, the forces of history that shape the flow of collective human destiny—that bring about the rise and fall of civilisations are economic in nature. These economic forces brought about the changes in society. Individuals were unimportant. *The forces of history were the tidal currents in the "racial unconscious" that relentlessly propelled the course of events.* Human beings were simply swept along with the flow of these forces. It was, therefore, important to analyse these forces, to understand their direction of flow. That was the path to social change. When this "change" was opposed by reactionary elements—it only served to build up the pressure of the social forces. This led to a violent dam burst or a bloody revolution in social terms. The individual was insignificant—the historical forces were paramount. We could easily replace the Marxist concept of the Forces of history (and the forces of economic change) with the forces (or the constructors) of species Evolution that guide not merely biological change but also social and cultural changes and scientific and technological development. Evolution then turns out to be not some random and erratic phenomena but a teleological and goal directed process. Modern viewpoints of evolution see it not as a graduated and incremental progression but as an episodic process. It seems to proceed in quantum jumps; long periods of stagnation and stability are followed by short periods of accelerated growth; by virtual quantum jumps in the collective consciousness. Thomas Kuhn who popularised the concept of the paradigm shift says, "Changes in Paradigms occur in discontinuous, revolutionary breaks called the Paradigm Shift".

*Toynbee's school represents the western viewpoint of history. It stressed that great leaders and empire builders have moulded the destinies of peoples.* One Alexander, a Caesar, a Genghis Khan, a Napoleon, a Bismarck or Hitler, a Roosevelt or Stalin, a Mao or Gandhi or Khomeini can leave an indelible stamp upon the collective destinies of mankind. The rise and fall of civilisation is the tale of the rise and fall of these titans. They do "bestride the narrow world like Colossuses" as long as they last. They leave an indelible imprint upon the history of mankind. These creative minorities provide the leadership that harmonises the collective energies of a people. This creative ability conferred upon them the leadership of the multitudes. Their personality traits were diverse, their personal qualities and lifestyles had nothing in common. *(The only thing that leaders have had in common is the fact that they all had followers)*. What is that magic, undeniable quality that makes a leader? *Social scientists have called this vague and indefinable leadership quality—CHARISMA*. It is this charisma that confers leadership. *The Buddha had it in a phenomenal measure, so did Jesus and Mohammed*. Their influence has reached out well beyond their life spans to influence the life styles of people thousands of years after their demise.

There were others like Alexander and Ashoka, Genghis Khan and Napoleon, Bismarck or Hitler, Castro and Khomeini who left an indelible impression upon the vast mass of mankind in their lifetimes. Recent studies on leadership abilities have sought to analyse this quality of charisma. *Most of these great leaders were great communicators. They were highly creative and gifted people*. Many of them have left behind or inspired vast volumes of writings. The founders of the great religions have inspired the sacred books of their people. *The Dharmapada, the Bible and the Koran are great attempts at a synthesis of the conventional wisdom of their age. They seek to provide an all-embracing ideology to guide their people. They seek to provide the overview or Paradigms for their respective cultures*. They seek to diagnose the ills of the human condition and prescribe simplistic remedies. These prophets and Christ figures are significant leadership phenomena whose image becomes a racial archetype, a powerful icon that reaches out across the eons of time to guide the destiny of a civilisation per se!

*Such charismatic leaders have the following outstanding traits*: —

(a) *Creative abilities* of a very high order. Many of them were prolific writers and left behind the philosophical overviews to guide their people. They inspired the sacred texts of the great world-religions.

(b) They possess tremendous *communication abilities*. Ann Arbor in her book "Spell Binders: Charismatic Political Leadership" feels that they are, in most cases, powerful demagogues. They are excellent at mobilising mass upsurges of emotions. The phenomenal rabble rousing abilities of Hitler or Khomeini are now part of legend and folklore. Their abilities to excite collective fears, and racial hatreds were hypnotic. Oratory and political rhetoric play an important part in such revivalist movements.

(c) *Powerful psychological insights into the cultural myths and mythology of their people. The myth is the basis of reality.* The racial myths are centred around the racial archetypes. An understanding of the "Weltanschauung" of a people leads to an ability to manipulate their mass feelings and emotions.

*Ann Arbor in her thoroughly researched book on charismatic leaders has stressed the importance of crisis or challenge in the rise of charismatic leaders.* After a study of nine recent charismatic leaders (to include Hitler, Mussolini, Castro, Mahatma Gandhi and Khomeini) she *concludes that such leaders have arisen only in a climate or culture of historical crisis or challenge.* Creative change only comes about in response to a challenge from the external social or natural environment. Toynbee too has stressed the importance of a challenge from the social or natural environment as the spur for the rise of great civilisations.

He has talked of the overwhelming contribution of the creative Minorities.

*The minority of creative leaders and a climate of crisis or environmental challenge that provokes them to generate a collective response are two halves of the same equation.* A systems view of the historical phenomena would recognise the interaction of the individual component with the collective whole. The creative leader actualises the neuron circuitry that mediates the new social philosophy or ideology or the scientific concepts that usher in the tides of change. The key to programming the other minds of the species then is language—the written or the spoken word serves to programme the human bio computers. Words can provoke the emotional response that the leader seeks to arouse. *The leader, therefore, must be a great communicator.* The role of oratory and political rhetoric are most significant. The leader must be aware of the existing memory content of the bio-computers he seeks to influence. Hence the crucial importance of his understanding of the cultural myths and of his people.

*The key human resources of any civilisation then are creativity and charisma. When a civilisation has a rich crop of creative individuals—its thinkers, scientists. Philosophers and integrators and its resources of charismatic leaders with excellent communication or programming skills; it thrives and prospers and profoundly influences all other cultures and races of the planet.* Creativity and charisma both are mediated by Neuro-physiological processes in the brain. They are the external manifestations of the deeper process of human evolution.

## Summary

Human creativity is the manifestation of the process of human evolution. Changes occur in the species in terms of creative responses to the challenges from the social and natural environment. Such creative responses are usually mediated in a few selective brains endowed with liberal supplies of neural energy practically in the form of glial cells to burn the glucose fuels that power the human bio-computer and specifically on new neuron-circuitry that mediates the radical new concepts and ideas.

An analysis of the act of creation highlights the mechanisms of creativity. Koestler has called this "Bisosciation". In conceptual terms it implies the ability to take a lateral leap or a "quantum jump" between two diverse logic chains or thought matrices. It is the ability to see new relationships and connections.

A neuro-physiological interpretation of this model of creativity indicates that the creative process involves the actualisation of new neural connections. *To understand this etching of new circuits we must delve into the chemistry of neuron transmitters and understand the language of "neuron-speak".* The triggers of change are these neuro-transmitters. At this stage it is important to understand a new paradigm that is emerging as a result of the application of the systems viewpoint to Biology. Rupert Sheldrake has postulated the concept of a collective species "field", which he calls the Morphogenetic Field. It seems to hint at a "hologramic relationship" between the individual brains and the collective species' morphogenetic field. A new skill learnt by one brain or a new concept actualised in one mind seems to diffuse and spread instantly through out the species' morphogenetic field. The inverse square law does not seem to operate in these field propagation phenomena. A skill once learnt by a set of control rats is learnt with demonstrably greater ease by any and every other rat in the world. This could be the basis of the anomalous phenomena of consciousness, which are currently in the realm of extra sensory perception. They deal with the non-localisation of consciousness and its amazing extension in space and time. Mankind has yet to come to terms with the full philosophical impact of this new paradigm. It will be taken up in greater detail in chapter nine.

Creativity, therefore, is the first key resource of any society. Civilisations rise when they are able to produce and nurture such creative minorities in conditions conducive to promoting the creative process. These conditions are provided by leisure. Leisure that conserves human energies otherwise wasted in routine chores for creative problem solving pursuits. *Leisure frees the creative individual from a linear view of time into a cyclical view; a cyclical view that enables him to break free from the linear-sequential-chains of logic—to take the quantum leaps and lateral jumps that inter-relate diverse matrices of thought.* The creative changes actualised in these minds are propagated throughout the species Morphogenetic field in a sub-conscious manner. They enter the collective racial unconscious through the gates of receptive individual minds. These new circuits however, still need to be propagated to other brains through the medium of language; for language serves to programme the bio-computer of the human brain. *Communication abilities then are a great adjunct to creativity—the language process can only transmit creative changes.* So a great civilisation needs a brilliant minority of creative individuals. *It also needs communicators to spread the creative concepts actualised* by these creative minds. Very often the creative person and the communicator are one and the same person. Communication abilities often seem to go hand in hand with creative abilities.

This brings us to a *supreme trinity of creativity, communication and CHARISMA.* All great world civilisations have been put on the path to glory and greatness by great charismatic leaders. These may have been religious or political leaders (very often in the past the two have fused in the same person). These brilliant creative and charismatic leaders have laid the foundations of great empires and cultures and world religions that moulded the destinies of mankind.

The two schools of history may put varying degrees of emphasis on the importance of the individual versus the subterranean forces of history or social change. Marxist Historians would stress the importance of the forces of history and underplay the contribution of the individual in shaping collective human destinies. Historians of Toynbee's school would go to the other extreme and extol the great leaders or the great Captains of War or the empire builders. The impact of their personalities was overriding and decisive. It is they who moulded history. They were not moulded or swept along by the tides of history.

Perhaps both schools of thought are equally right. For they are each stressing one half of a unitary equation. The individual mind and the collective Morphogenetic field are linked in a symbiotic or hologramic relationship. The whole is a sum total of the parts—the parts in turn CONTAIN the whole. *Charismatic leaders have arisen only in situations of great crisis or challenge. The forces of history are not merely economic but evolutionary in nature.* They represent the collective conditions of the species morphogenetic field. They are expressed strongly through individual minds that are most receptive to such changes. Through these minds they are verbalised and spread as complete "field programmes" (ideologies) to influence entire cultures and civilisations. Civilisations however, would not have paid heed to these verbal inputs were they not already in a receptive condition as a collectivity. Such works help only when the human bio-computers in general are in a susceptible or receptive condition, then they spread like wildfire. Toynbee had correctly highlighted the role of challenge from the social or physical environment and the response by the creative minorities.

## The Avatar Theory

*This idea is very aptly highlighted by the Indian philosophical work of the Gita. It propagates the theory of "Avatara" or highly gifted and charismatic beings, who "incarnate" or arise whenever there is a great decline in the human condition.*

(Yada-Yada hi dharmasya"—i.e., whenever righteousness declines). There is, therefore, a *complementary relationship between a situation of great challenge from the social, cultural or natural environment and the emergence of a towering charismatic leader—a powerful personality that leaves its indelible impress upon the times.* These charismatic beings are cultural revivalists and great integrators or synthesisers of the existing traditions. They provide the ideological guidance to their race through its periods of unrest and transition. The revivalists are called Avatars in the Indian philosophical traditions. The universal condition of decline and the emergence of a great leader therefore are a deeply inter-related phenomena. They are part of the same systems view of historical change. The one is incomplete without the other. The remarkable feature of the Avatara theory is its suggestion that these *civilisational icons and Avatars were beings in whom the Kundalini energy was fully kinetised and awakened.* The rise of the Kala Agni—reversed the arrow of time in their beings and made them such great visionaries and prophets. They foresaw the future and acted in the present to actualise its impending potentials.

# CHAPTER THREE

## INDIAN CONCEPTS OF CREATIVITY: THE KUNDALINI

The ancient *Indian civilisation viewed the human creative resources with awe and reverence. It deified this creative faculty and worshipped it both in its individual and universal aspects.* It defied the creative intelligence and worshipped it as its ruling deity. *The Gayatri Mantra (Hymn)—the most sacred verse of the Rig Veda addresses this inner resource as the "internal sun that illumines our inner space. (Aditi—*the mother of the sun is the symbol of space). The hymn says: *"We meditate upon the ineffable effulgence of THAT resplendent sun. May that sun illumine our intelligence for the good of all living beings".*

The sun incidentally *is the sub conscious symbol of the human libido.* In the Freudian interpretation, the sun appears in our dreams as the symbol of our sexuality. The sun referred to in the hymn was THAT sun—that blazing symbol of the creative intelligence—the symbol of fusion and synthesis. *Hydrogen atoms fuse into Helium in the core of the sun and make it shine in all its brilliance. Ideas and concepts fuse in the creative intelligence and lend it intellectual brilliance.*

The Indian Tantric tradition was even more blatantly explicit in its symbolism. Sir John Woodroffe has done much to popularise the Indian icon of the Kundalini—the coiled—serpent energy—the theoretical basis of all human creativity. Creativity that is expressed physiologically as sexuality—as the reproductive mechanism of the species and in psychological terms as the creative— intelligence that brings about our marvellous insights and intuitions. It universalised this creative faculty as the *"shakti"*—the creative energy—the mother or the matrix of the universe. Tantric literature went into a mass of physiological details about this creative mechanism in the human species. Its libidinous character is blatantly proclaimed by the explicitly sexual tantric motifs—the phallic symbols and representations of the human genitalia. *The Kundalini therefore had a lot in common with the Freudian concept of the libido.* To be specific it was *more in tune with Jung's conception of the Libido* (for Jung and Freud had differed over the basic nature of the Libido). Sigmund Freud had viewed the Libido as a "chemical tension", a bio-chemically induced itch that had to be scratched. It was a more empirical view. Jung in harmony with Robert Myers conception in the field of physics *took an "Energic" view of the Libido*—as a more generalised creative energy resource rather than a highly particularised and specifically sexual mechanism.

As per the Tantric tradition, the Kundalini is the coiled up creative energy that lies dormant at the base of the human spine. It is called the serpent energy. It is the energy that "created" the human organism and then has gone into dormant or "potential" condition. This energy helps mankind to reproduce itself. If made to flow "upwards" (*Urdhva Retas*) it aids in the evolution of the organism. Tantric literature goes into great details about a network of *Nadis* in the human energy field and the body. These are quite akin to the "chi channels" or meridians of Acupuncture. In the main there are three channels: 1. The central channel of the Sushumna (some equate it with the Central Nervous System); 2. The Pingala or the hot solar channel (this is often equated with the sympathetic nervous system); 3. The Ida or the lunar channel (which is equate with the Parasympathetic nervous system). The Tantras describe seven centres of consciousness in the human energy field. These are called the chakras or the wheels. In the human body their locations correspond with the Nerve plexuses and the Endocrine Glands. The Kundalini is the residual energy of creation that lies dormant at the terminal end of the spine. It is aroused and kinetised. It then rises, piercing through chakra after chakra till it reaches the Seventh Chakra of the *Sahasrar* in the Brain. That leads to liberation, to Moksha to the Nirvana experience of great ecstasy, infinitude and overwhelming reality.

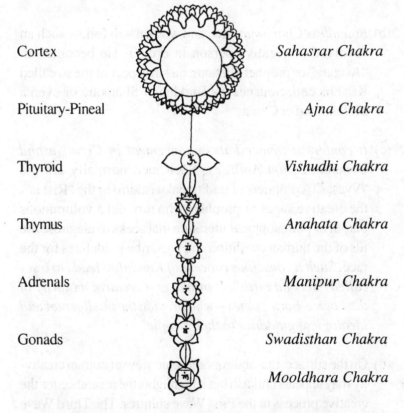

| | |
|---|---|
| Cortex | *Sahasrar Chakra* |
| Pituitary-Pineal | *Ajna Chakra* |
| Thyroid | *Vishudhi Chakra* |
| Thymus | *Anahata Chakra* |
| Adrenals | *Manipur Chakra* |
| Gonads | *Swadisthan Chakra* |
| | *Mooldhara Chakra* |

Its arousal confers significant gifts upon the person who succeeds in such an "arousal". In the main it is supposed to confer: —

(a) *An Inexpressible Ecstasy*: the highest tactile reward known
to man—the experience of "Sat-Chit-Ananda"—the core
mystical experience of the ultimate merger of the individual
being in the universal consciousness: the so called Nirvana or
Moksha experience that leads to a feeling of oceanic expansion of consciousness. The intense tactical rewards of this
orgiastic experience, it is said, far supersede the tactical rewards of the reproductive process. It brings about a significantly altered state of consciousness.

(b) *Boundless Charisma:* Men and women will follow such an
"evolved or creative person in droves. He becomes an
"Avatara" or prophet phenomena (an aspect of the so called
Krishna consciousness) a Buddha or Shankara or even a
Mohammed or Christ.

(c) *It confers a tremendous enhancement in Creative and
Communication Abilities:* Such men normally are the
"Vyasas" (compilers of traditional wisdom) or the "Rishis",
the creative sages or prophets who turn out a voluminous
output of philosophical literature that seeks to diagnose the
ills of the human condition and prescribe guidelines for the
race. *Such a conscious process of Kundalini leads to a so-
called "second birth". It produces a creative minority of
the "twice-born" elites—who provide the intellectual and
ideological guidance to their people.*

(d) On the surface, this anthropomorphic view of human creativity may appears childish but it highlights the reverence for the
creative process in the First Wave cultures. The Third Wave
civilisation will have to lay an equally heavy emphasis on the
cultivation and conscious promotion of human creative abilities. It will have to worship creativity even as the ancient First

Wave cultures did. But first it will have to unravel and understand the true nature and mechanism of human creativity. It is here that the primitive Indian Vedic and Tantric conceptions provide significant clues that can now be reinterpreted in terms of the modern knowledge of human physiology.

It is possible that the Kundalini motif that has become a racial icon for the Indian people is a prefect example of dynamic inventiveness. Kekule visualised the structure of the Benzene molecule in a dream. He visualised a snake biting its own tail. This dream symbol provided a powerful insight that enabled him to unravel the ring structure of the Benzene molecule. It is fascinating to speculate that the Kundalini motif itself is such an imagic insight. It is a symbol that can help us to unravel the secrets of human creativity. This symbol cannot obviously be taken literally but has to be analysed and reflected upon to yield the scientific parallels that it is pointing out.

It is possible that the Kundalini motif perhaps represents symbolical insights into the nature of human creativity. *It is possible that the Kundalini is perhaps a symbol of the sublimated human libido.* The inverted direction (*Urdhava Retas*) seems to indicate a mobilisation of human sexuality from the normal purposes of procreation to the "higher" purposes of evolution. Hence the "upward" directional thrust. The direction is perhaps metaphorical. There are a number of interesting facets of the Kundalini theory that merit a deeper reflection. *The Kundalini is said to be the energy that brings about the birth of the organism and then becomes dormant. It is "coiled" up like a serpent. Its remobilisation represents a "second birth". The "birth" analogy and the coiled up structure are highly significant clues.* Were the ancient philosophers vaguely trying to express intuitive insights, which they could not accurately interpret due to the primitive state of their physiological and scientific knowledge? There are a number of symbols or parallelism that could help us to reinterpret this theory of creativity in modern neuro-physiological terms.

*Kundalini—the coiled one—the serpentine energy could well be a subconscious symbol for the coiled up Double Helix structure of the DNA—the basic blue prints of life and heredity.*

The Kundalini's symbol of two serpents coiled about one another is remarkably similar to the Double Helix spiral structure of the DNA molecule. This itself is the most significant clue to what is implied by the symbols.

The Tantric texts dwell in very great detail upon a network of *nadis* or nerve channels through which this creative energy is supposed to operate. *There is the Sushumna or the central channel that runs along the length of the spine.* It is supposed to be dormant in normal conditions. The Kundalini energy "opens" this channel. *There is the Pingala or the "hot" solar channel, which runs on the Right side and the "Ida" or the "cold" lunar channel which runs along the left of the spinal column as* described in Tantric texts. The points of junction of the three nerve channels form *the chakras—the wheels or the centres of "creative energy".* There are a total of seven such chakras or centres in the body. Viewed superficially this description seems archaic and fanciful. But reinterpreted in the light of modern physiology, *these chakras sites closely correspond to the nerve plexuses* namely the Thoracic plexus, the Cardiac plexus and the Solar and Sacral plexuses. Even more significantly, *these so called chakras correspond in location with the endocrine glands.* The chart below indicates this "site correspondence".

| CHAKRA | CORRESPONDING PLEXUS | CORRESPONDING ENDOCRINE GLAND |
|---|---|---|
| Sahasrar | | Pineal Gland |
| Ajna | | Pituitary Gland |
| Vishuddhi | Thoracic Plexus | Thyroid Gland |
| Anahata | Cardiac Plexus | Thymus Gland |
| Manipura | Solar Plexus | Adrenal Glands Pancreas |
| Swadisthana | | Ovaries/Testes |
| Mooldhara | Sacral Plexus | |

*The Nadi Network of the Indian Tantric texts has close parallels with the channels or meridians mentioned in the Chinese Acupuncture texts.* At the physiological level—the correspondence between this symbolic arrangement and the human nervous system comprising of the central nervous system and the sympathetic and para-sympathetic nervous system is striking. Location and description wise the Sushumna could well correspond to the CNS, the Pingla to the Sympathetic and the Ida to Parasympathetic nervous systems. The ancient map of the nerve network can then be viewed as a symbolic representation of the central and peripheral nervous systems.

## Heat and Cold: The Solar and Lunar Nerves

The Hot and Cold aspect that has been stressed has a symbolic significance again. The Pingla nerve channel is said to be hot and the Ida channel is the cold nerve channel. These are subconscious symbols that have to be reinterpreted in physiological terms. There are some very interesting parallels with the heat and cold aspect. Some decades ago *Dr. Stanley Jones had presented a paper of the "Thermostatic Theory of the Biological origin of Emotions"* at the Loyalla Symposium. Dr. Jones had postulated that *the basic emotions of rage and lust are the outgrowth of the mammalian response to heat and cold.* Now in mammals defence against cold is mobilised by the Sympathetic nervous system by constricting the blood vessels and increasing the thermal output of the heart. *The Sympathetic nervous system then could be symbolised by the 'hot' solar channel or the Pingala of the tantric texts.* Incidentally the same biological mechanism is responsible for mediating not just reaction against cold but also in expressing the emotion of rage. The cardio-vascular components of the rage reaction are acceleration of the heart and constriction of the blood vessels; it is characterised by a rise in the blood pressure and over activity of the anti gravity muscles. All these are mediated by the Sympathetic Nervous System.

*The Parasympathetic nervous system on the other hand mobilises the body's defence against heat. This is done by a slowing of heart and vasodilatation. To that extent the "Ida" or the "cold" Lunar channel of the Tantric texts may correspond to the Para-sympathetic nervous system.* Jones went on to postulate that the same mammalian response to heat was also the physiological mechanism of the emotion of lust. *Lust is said to be a para-sympathetic emotion necessitating dilation of blood vessels.* This dilation is brought about by the parasympathetic nervous system in general and the vagus nerve in particular. (However the situation here is a bit more complex as the action of the parasympathetic nervous system in mediating lust has to be in constructive opposition to the action of the Sympathetic nervous system).

Here we have a viable physiological basis that could help to interpret the symbolism of the hot and cold "nadi" channels. We also have a clear relationship between this biological mechanism and the basic human emotions of rage and lust. The primary emotion of love and hate are, therefore founded on the physiological reaction of lust and rage. Lust and rage are not "affect" or feelings but are seen even in decerebrate cats and dogs—animals bereft of their cerebral cortex and in whom therefore, there is no question of affect or feeling. The physiological aspects of our emotions are made operative through the two halves of the autonomic nervous system.

*The two halves of the autonomic nervous system have their headquarters in the hypothalamus* (that is situated between the two lobes of the brain). The Sympathetic in the Posterior (or rear) hypothalamus and the Parasympathetic in the Anterior (or frontal hypothalamus. *The hypothalamus functions as a sea-saw, an either—or mechanism (an OR gate in terms of computer circuitry). The primary homeostasis function of the hypothalamus and autonomic nervous system is temperature control.* Defence against cold being mobilised by the rear hypothalamus and the Sympathetic nervous system by constriction of blood vessels and increasing the thermal output of the heart. Defence against heat is mobilised by the anterior hypothalamus and the para-sympathetic nervous system by vasodilatation. The same mechanism is operative in the display of emotions.

The hypothalamus is a significant thermostat of the human body. It is responsible for the preservation of the constancy of the internal environment. This it does by: —

(1) **Glucostasis**: The balance of the antagonism of Adrenalin and Insulin.

(2) **Thermostasis**: Balance of Vasodilatation and Vasoconstriction.

(3) **Emotional Homeostasis**: Balance of Lust and rage and therefore of Love and Hate.

Thus we find that there are significant correlations between temperature control and our autonomic nervous system. To that extent the Pingla or sympathetic nervous system may well be deemed "hot" and the Ida or parasympathetic as "cold".

This temperature aspect occurs time and again in the Kundalini process. It is recorded that persons undergoing this process have sometimes experienced intense burning sensations (as if they have been set alight by an internal fire). Those who have successfully completed this inner transformation process report an indifference to heat and cold. All this points to a significant involvement of the hypothalamus and the peripheral nervous systems in the process.

## The Serpent Symbolism: Reptilian Structures of the Brain

The serpent symbolism is twofold. It is possibly a most obvious symbol of the DNA—the basic building blocks of life in the nuclei of our cells. Many tantric texts represent the Kundalini in the form of two snakes coiled about one another as shown in the diagram.

Compare this with the Double Helix Spiral structure of the DNA Molecule as expressed by the Francis—Crick—Watson model. The similarity is so marked that it is astounding.

Besides this correspondence at the molecular level, *the basis of much of the action ascribed to the Kundalini is in the ancient Reptilian core of the human brain.* The human brain may very superficially be divided into the new brain (comprising the cerebral cortex) and the old brain or *the ancient Reptilian brain comprising of the brain stem, the hypothalamus, thalamus and the limbic system.* These are the more archaic parts of mans evolutionary acquisition. Yet *these archaic structures have more direct access to mans central and autonomic nervous system and hence far greater control over the states of the body than the newer cortex.* Perhaps this crudely explains why our emotions, (which are largely mediated through the ancient reptilian brain structures and the central and autonomic nervous system) hold more sway on man than his reason which operates through the cortex alone. (True higher emotions are also mediated through the cortex—but the expression of emotions is largely the domain of the ancient reptilian structures of the human brain). *This reptilian core of the human brain and not the terminal end of the human spine may well be the real seat of the Kundalini—the creative energy in our bodies.*

The snake therefore is the most apt symbol of the libidinal energy that lies at the core of a man's aliveness. This "serpent energy"—this core of sexual and emotional drives is the basic powerhouse of the human organism. The Mythological Serpent of paradise that tempted Eve in the Garden of Eden was this "Libidinal Serpent". The serpent symbolism is most apt. It directly and specifically points out to the ancient reptilian structures that constitute the core of man's brain.

## The Metaphor of Birth and Residual Potential

The third significant clue about the specific physiological nature of the so-called Kundalini or creative energy mechanism is provided by the symbol of birth. The man in whom the Kundalini was active was said to have undergone a "second birth". He was there after referred to as the *Dvij* or "twice born". The process of the generation of a human being from the single fertilized cell encapsulate as it were the millenniums of evolution in a process of "burst communication". For deciphering this clue we have to fall back to the science of Embryology. Before we take up the parallel let us examine the mythological symbols in greater detail. *The subconscious mind cannot hold abstract concepts. It must hold them in imagic form—in the form of subconscious symbols.* Some of these symbols are racial Archetypes—they are common to an entire people. It is possible that these could be genetically transmitted through the centuries and comprises the collective "script" or "Weltanschauung" of the race.

The mythology of a people then holds invaluable clues to their psychological make up. The myth is indeed the basis of reality. The motifs of the Kundalini myth hold significant clues to the real nature of the phenomena of creativity. In Indian Mythology—Vishnu (the Lord of the Mind) after having created the Cosmos rests upon the seat of the mighty, thousand hooded serpent that floats upon the surface of the cosmic ocean. This fairy tale picture has now to be analysed for its symbolical clues. Vishnu represents the mind—the cerebral Cortex—the intelligence of man. The Serpent represents the ancient reptilian structures of the brain through which the creative emotional—sexual energies are mediated. *The ocean represents consciousness. Even otherwise the brain floats in the buffer of spinal fluid. This thousand-hooded serpent of Indian mythology is called the Shesha-Naga. The word "Shesha" means "Residual" or "Left over". Reinterpreted this myth means that the creative energy that is responsible for the birth of the human organism rests in the mind. It is active at the time of the growth of the embryo. Having formed the foetus into the newborn child it gradually becomes latent. It then remains in the reptilian brain as latent potential.* It is this latent genetic potential that can also reproduce the organism.

It is this energic latent energy that can be mobilised for other creative pursuits. No creative activity is possible unless this creative energy complex powers it. The process of the growth of the embryo encapsulates the history of human evolution. It is played out at a rapid and accelerated rate in the womb. The science of embryology provides us very significant clues about the real nature of this creative mechanism. Let us therefore analyse the process of birth. The male sperm fertilizes the ovum or the egg cell of the female. *This single fertilized cell contain the entire genetic code that can give rise to a six foot tall wrestler with jet black hair and a dimple on his chin.* The nucleus of the fertilized cell contains the total genetic potential for such a transformation. This single fertilized cell multiples and grows in the womb by the process of cellular fission—the division and multiplication of cells. ("I am one—let me be many", assertion of the Upanishads is significant in this regard). A few weeks after conception—the first organ specific zones appear in the embryo. These are called the morphogenetic zones. They will give rise to the many organs of the body—the eyes, the ears, the heart, lungs, kidneys, liver, pancreas, etc. These zones are organ specific. Experiments conducted on Salamander embryo have proved that if one cell of the eye zone is grafted on to the belly region of another salamander foetus it will grow an eye lens there. This organ specialisation can only be achieved by blocking the remainder genetic potential of the cell. This specialisation is region and form specific and is a process of tunnelisation. It blocks out all the other aspects to permit only that organ specific potential to actualise. In the eye cells all the other genetic potential is blocked to enable only the eye aspect to emerge and grow. *Thus organs are created not so much by a process of construction as by a process of control or blocking of irrelevant genetic potentials.* These organ specific zones are independent or semi-autonomous hierarchies. They grow on their own, without waiting for a special trigger signal or initiating impulses from the foetal brain. In fact the organ development starts well before the foetal brain is fully formed. Each of these organ specific zones develops autonomously. Arthur Koestler has called such autonomous hierarchies—"Holons". It is only later that they come under the overall suzerainty of the brain. Thus the cells of the heart zone specialise to produce the foetal heart, those of the eye zone the foetal eye lenses and so on.

   This organ specialisation is an exclusive process. It occurs at a cost—at the cost of blocking all the remainder genetic potential of the cell to permit the specific organ potential alone to manifest. Reality is constructed through such "filters" or "gates".

   *Arthur Koestler has said in his magnum opus (The Act of Creation) that the only cells that retain their full genetic potential (their pristine genetic toti-potentiality) are the cells of the reproductive system.* For it is these cells that ensure the propagation of the species. To recreate in full they must retain the full genetic potential to spawn the entire organism. Being "generalist" cells they are spared the controls, filters and blockages of the process of specialisation. *Arthur Koestler has suggested that these toti-potential cells could serve as the triggers for initiating the process of evolution.* The core of the reproductive system incidentally is in the brain, in the hypothalamus and pituitary master gland. Perhaps the crucial issue is not so much the localisation of the triggers cells—*but the underlying programming mechanism that blocks and releases the genetic potentials. The process of evolution then would imply a release of blocked or latent genetic potentials.* The Kundalini—the coiled one—the serpent energy—is the energy of these latent genetic potentials—these latent potentialities and "bio-computer programmes"; these latent probabilities that can be actualised only through the gates and filters of this control mechanism. What then is this central control mechanism? What is the nature of this invisible programming component, this "ghost in the machine"?

   *A programmed release of these genetic controls could bring about species evolution—an erratic release of these genetic controls on the other hand could lead to cancer.* Since these phenomena occur at the genetic level their hereditary transmission is axiomatic (Evolution proceeds through changes that are genetically transferable to the off spring). We can now highlight obvious parallels between these latent genetic potentials of the reproductive cells and the latent ("Shesha") or residual nature of the creative energy concept of Hindu mythology.

We are today at the threshold of a major revolution in our scientific paradigms. *So far microbiology has remained the last bastion of classical Newtonian physics. It is still fixated upon the outdated concepts of Particle Physics—whereas physics itself has graduated to a field view of reality.* A most significant revolution in our worldview will occur once we apply the concepts of quantum mechanical thought to the field of microbiology. There is therefore, *an urgent need to synthesise the New Physics with the Life Sciences.* There is a need to break the particle fixation of the life sciences, for this fixation is a dangerous anachronism in the Third Wave. The sciences must adopt a systems view of the phenomena of life. The development of science has witnessed the synthesis of electricity and magnetism and then the strong and weak forces. Physics is pushing towards a final synthesis between the four basic forces (electro-magnetic, gravitational, strong and weak). But the grandest synthesis of all will be the unification of physics with Life Sciences.

## Informational Energy Fields

Such a bold step was long overdue. But it has since been taken. *In a paper entitled "A new Paradigm for the Reunification of Science", Dr. Victor Benedict Arul—an Indian micro-biologist* working in the USA has made a significant attempt to *synthesise the Life Sciences with the New Physics. He has applied the mathematical tenets of the information theory to living systems.* It all began as an attempt to unravel the causes of cancer but has led us to the contours of an exciting and breathtakingly new paradigm that could exorcise the Life Sciences of their mechanistic fixation.

*Dr. Arul has proposed the existence of an "Informational Bio-energy complex" existing in space—bio-energy that serves as the blue print of life. He calls it the Informational energy field. It is this field that provides the informational stimuli for organising the cells of the living organism.* These informational fields are the bio energic matrices (or Force—Field blue prints) that serve as the building blocks of life. They provide the informational inputs that trigger the growth of cells and determine the shape and structure of the living organisms. *Dr. Arul posits that cancer occurs when the informational inputs from the field are blocked in a particular organ of the body. In the absence of these organising inputs the cells begin to grow erratically and haphazardly—thus leading to cancer.*

The Field view is finding an increasing number of adherents. We have already mentioned the Morphogenetic Field theorised by Dr. Rupert Sheldrake. The Soviets too have been talking *of Bio-plasma as a theoretical fourth state of matter.* Extensive research on "Kiralian Auras" was carried out in the Soviet Union some years back and generated a lot of controversy. Perhaps we are at the threshold of a significant paradigm shift. *The Indian philosophers had theorised about "Prana" to explain the energic basis of the Kundalini.* The Prana concept bears a very striking resemblance to the Informational Energy Field concept. In all explanations of the action of the Kundalini—the ancient Indian philosophers relied upon the concept of Prana or Life-energy. This appeared a primitive theory that smacked of the cardinal scientific sin of "vitalism". But with the approaching paradigm shift in Biology from a particle fixation to a field view—"Prana" may not appear such a ludicrous conception after all. The concept of the informational—energy field or Morphogenetic Field is bound to cause a significant revolution in our world view. Rupert

Sheldrake had posited the theory of the Morphogenetic Fields in his Magnum opus, "A New Science of Life". His Morphogenetic Fields are curiously similar to the Soma Fields and Pranic fields of Indian Philosophy. A Magnetic Field cannot exist in the absence of a magnet that generates it. Morphogenetic fields however are different. They are the form generating fields. They exist per se and are the cause of the generation of life forms. They take over the evolution of the single fertilised egg cell in the womb and cause it to grow as per a pre-existing format and design. The guiding trigger and filter signals that operate the uplifting of the genetic programme in the fertilised cell, all originate from this form-generating field. These form-generating fields provide the basic blue prints that guide the unfolding of the super structure of the Bones (the skeletal system), the nervous system, the blood and lymph circulatory system and the Immune system. Viewed in this light, the ancient analogies now make more sense. The informational order, on which our organisms are based, is housed in the Morphogenetic fields, which serve as the blue prints of life. The Morphogenetic fields that surround all living things contain the entire programme for generating the human organism and its sub systems is localised in this field. It is *transmitted through coded instructions at the genetic level. The orchestra of endocrine glands mediates it in the body.* We can see the whole process in a highly activated stage in the process of the formation of and growth of an embryo. For a few years after birth the process continues at this accelerated pace of metabolism. Then it slips into a latent stage.

*The organism becomes hyper active again at the stage of Puberty. We see another instalment of release from the "Field Programme". The trigger signals are received at the hypo-thalamus and at the endocrine glands to commence secretion of trigger enzymes and neuro-transmitters.* The bio-chemical dynamo hums at full power to achieve the transformation. As per the Indian system it can artificially be activated yet again in a metaphorical process of a "second birth" that enhances creative intelligence, communication abilities and charisma. The unleashing of this latent programme at the genetic level is described as the activation of the Kundalini.

## The Problem of Form

Life forms are vastly different from material or mechanical forms. The structure of the atom and molecules in a cycle or car is quite rigidly fixed. It does not change over time. A Life form is radically different. The "form" remains constant, even as the atoms and molecules are constantly replaced. Every 10 years all the atoms in our face are changed. How then do they retain the same form? The solution to this problem has been posited in terms of the form generating Morphogenetic field. Living systems therefore are like whirlpools. The form of the whirlpool remains constant even as the water in the whirlpool is forever changing.

## Morphic Resonance

Just as crystals always crystallise in a particular ways, most life forms unfold as per the acquired patterns of past evolution. This occurs by what Sheldrake has termed the process of Morphic resonance. Just as a life form is about to unfold itself, information about the past unfolding of such forms steps across quantum mechanically from the past to guide the unfolding of the new form as per the past pattern. The Morphogenetic fields therefore are the form generating fields that are the causative agents of the development and maintenance of Biological form.

## Summary

A unique feature of the Ancient First Wave Civilisation in India was its glorification of creativity. It placed the human creative faculty on a divine—trans-human pedestal. The Kundalini conception of this creative energy seemed to chart an empirical course for the maximisation of this human creative resource. The process of so-called "arousal" of the Kundalini charts a detailed course for the development and unfolding of this latent potential in the species.

*The Kundalini icon is a powerful racial symbol. It is, perhaps a symbol of the sublimated Libido.* Its serpentine, coiled shape has very striking parallels with the coiled Double Helix structure of the DNA. This resemblance seems to indicate that the Kundalini creative energy being invoked was a genetic trigger mechanism that led to the unfolding of latent genetic potentials. The release of genetic controls as per a "pre-wired" programme could lead to an evolutionary growth of the species—an evolutionary growth that could be genetically transmitted to the offspring. An uncontrolled or riotous release could lead to cancer. This hypothesis is best understood in terms of an emerging field view of life. *This hypothesis requires the acceptance of an "Informational Energy Field" or Morphogenetic field that exists in space—bio energy. All the informational inputs—the trigger signals—the blocking signals or control and filter signals originate in this Morphogenetic field and manipulate the molecular level of life at the level of the DNA and RNA itself.* Such a Field or systems view of the living organisms will engender a sweeping revolution in the science of Biotechnology. And Biotechnology indeed is the science of the organic cultures that will emerge in the Third Wave civilisation. *A synthesis of Biotechnology and electronics may well lead to the birth of a glorious new science. We could call it the science of BIONICS.* Classical Newtonian physics sought seed ideas in Greek philosophy and mysticism. Modern physicists like Fritjof Capra are already turning to oriental mysticism to provide the doctrinal and conceptual inspirations that will perhaps lead to significant break through in establishing new scientific paradigms.

# CHAPTER FOUR

## SUPER CHARISMA: THE AVATARA THEORY AND THE KUNDALINI

The entire gamut of the foregoing discussion—the concepts of the Informational Energy Fields or Morphogenetic field are all in the nature of philosophical speculation. They are theories, which remain to be verified fully under laboratory conditions. But they do point out to the direction that research is now taking at its foremost fringes. They also establish the areas that we must emphasise in our future research efforts to enhance our understanding of reality.

To get to the unknown we have to build bridges from the known. In order to speculate about the true nature of reality we have to proceed from what we do know as facts. The unknown however, can only be known once we have generated a mind map of that reality—once we have constructed a hypothesis or a theory about what it is like. Only then can we proceed with repeatable experiments, to establish the truth of our hypothesis. That is the scientific method, as we know it. Why should we waste research endeavours on an archaic and primitive theory that can at best provide vague clues and symbols about the human creative mechanism? The Kundalini hypothesis would not merit scientific scrutiny were it not for the fact that *the Tantric-Yogic texts outline a definite programme of repeatable psychosomatic exercises with the aid of which this process can be unleashed in any mature human organism.* These involve *esoteric exercises in concentration (directed-attention) and meditation.* However, the value of the Kundalini hypothesis goes beyond this prescriptive base. *There exists a considerable data bank of the physiological changes that such a process unleashes in human beings.* It is this fact that makes it a worthwhile research subject. The recorded cases of such successful "Kundalini arousals" have been very few and far in between. They have been extremely rare phenomena. The Indian First Wave civilisation had taken great pains to preserve such accounts for posterity. It had given greater reverence to its mystics than to its King -Emperors and great Captains of war. The Indian civilisation has taken great care to record the lives of these few such creative individuals as role models for the race. *The Vedas record the inspired verses of the primal Indian seers. Creativity and rhythmic speech appear to be the first gifts of this evolved or altered state of consciousness.* Ecstasy and rapture are its prime characteristics. Verse after verse in the Vedas records this joy and ecstasy, generated by the inner process of evolution. This ecstasy and peak experience was attributed to Soma. The mystical Soma that confers the gift of rapture and rhythmic speech (or poetry). It serves to enhance creativity by several orders of magnitude. The inner transformation of the experiencing consciousness is characterised by the onset of ecstasy, euphoria and grandiosity. It leads to an absence of fear. It leads to an incredible sensitivity to the aesthetic. The rarity of this phenomenon adds to its overwhelming significance. The Gita says, "Of the many thousands who set out to achieve it only some persevere; and of those who persevere only one meets with success". The Vedas mention long inner struggles, which are essential for the full onset of such an evolved consciousness. In the beginning it comes in flashes, as rays of luminosity that vanish that seem to be lost forever. One has to struggle to perfect the inner instrument that can continually express—this evolved consciousness. The lives of those who succeeded entirely in undergoing the inner unfolding of latent genetic potentials; served as evolutionary models for the race. Historical personages who underwent this revolutionary biological process of change and were able to live full and meaningful lives are extolled as the incarnations of Vishnu, Vishnu, the symbol of the mind, Vishnu, the symbol of the evolved consciousness and regeneration. *The motif of the playful Godchild Krishna symbolises the birth of a new consciousness.*

The penultimate development along the Kundalini trail therefore is the Avatara or the Buddhic being, a conception peculiar to the Indian civilisation. The Avatara represents the highest flowering of the human creative potentials. He is endowed with a super charisma that can mobilise a whole people and leave an indelible impact upon the course of history. This highly creative individual is a great synthesiser and cultural revivalist. The super charisma that he exhibits seems to be the chief expression of the unfolding of latent genetic potentials in the human species. Such a personage becomes a racial icon of sorts. He enters the collective unconscious of the people as a racial archetype. The entire mythology of the race is woven around him and his exploits. *The legends of Rama and Krishna have left an indelible stamp upon the consciousness of all South and South East Asia. Even today they form the main themes of all ballads and art and dance forms.* These cultural motifs are pivotal not only in India but in Thailand, Cambodia, Sri Lanka, Indonesia, Java, Sumatra and Bali. The myth is so overblown that it becomes difficult to separate the kernel of historical fact from legend and embellishment. In the Buddha however, we have such a powerful charismatic personality whose historical veracity is beyond doubt. Interestingly enough, he is part of the series of Hindu Avataras of Vishnu. These Avataras are supposed to be divine incarnations of godhead. Since the Atman—the individual entity is part of the Paramatman (or cosmic whole) human and divine are not distinct and inseparable entities in Indian philosophical thought. The activation of the Kundalini makes the human achieve divinity. The biographies of the later Avatars—Parashurama, Ram, Krishna and Gautama Buddha all speak of long years in forest exile that were spent in deep meditation and contemplation, psycho-somatic exercises that led to a full kinetisation of the Kundalini, to a rise of the Kala Agni that reversed the arrow of time in their beings and made them great visionaries and prophets (the Kala Purushas). The Hindu Avatars then returned to civilisation to lead their people in the political, cultural and military spheres. The Buddha returned to spread his universal doctrine of "Dharma". He established the "Sangha" and his disciples spread the Buddhist ideology over the whole of Asia.

**The Avatara Theory:** The theory of divine incarnation points to an interesting concept of human history. Thus Krishna—the author of the Gita declares that whenever righteousness (Dharma) declines and evil prevails, he incarnates to rectify the ills of the human condition. Here we find a curious and *unintended synthesis of the Marxist and the Toynbee schools of history. The forces of history represent the condition of a general decline in the state of human affairs.* They provide conditions of great challenge from the social and natural environments. Only in such turbulent conditions do we find a great one, a powerful and charismatic leader, a great communicator and ideologue arise amidst the people. He is the *fully evolved being who provides a role model or exemplar for his people, a powerful prophet of new ideas who leads his people to a chosen land* so to speak. History hangs upon his every word and syllable, his every thought and action for he represents the role model or exemplar for his age.

*Extrapolate this Avatara theory beyond the Indian civilisation and it could equally fit a Moses or Christ, a Mohammed or a Zoroaster.* The Buddha—the Shakya Muni incidentally is already regarded as one of the incarnations of this Vishnu consciousness. In Buddhistic thought the Avatara series is replaced by the concept of Bodhisattvas.

The Avatara theory should be of deep interest to evolution-ists. The Puranic lore in India records ten incarnations of this Vishnu or evolved consciousness (one of whom is yet to come). *The series of these incarnations follows a very curious progression along the evolutionary ladder.* J B S Haldane had noted this strong correspondence many decades ago. It would be interesting to trace this succession of "Avataras" or incarnations.

(1) **Matsya Avatara.** The first Avatara of Vishnu is recorded as appearing in the form of a gigantic White fish. Life began in the marine environs. The great White Whale, the Moby Dick like leviathan seems to represent an archetypal symbol in the collective unconscious of the human race. The myth of the great flood is common to many cultures. A curious fact about this white whale was its ability to grow at will almost overnight into gigantic proportions. It could accelerate its genetic potentials and grow at a fantastic rate as per the myth. Such a being could exercise a conscious control over his genetic processes as per this myth. The great white leviathan of the deep uncharted realms is an archetypal symbol from the collective unconscious of the human race. It is regarded as the first incarnation of the Vishnu consciousness. It saved mankind from an epochal flood (possibly caused by a bout of global warming).

(2) **The Kurma Avatara:** Interestingly enough the next incarnation of this evolved or Vishnu consciousness emerges as a gigantic Tortoise. Here we have reached the evolutionary level of the amphibian—life reaching out from the sea to the land. The gigantic size continues to highlight the genetic mechanism entailed in this evolutionary process as it were. The Kurma incarnation provided the base for the churning of the ocean of consciousness by the Forces of light and the forces of darkness.

(3) **The Varaha Avatara:** Here "Vishnu" appears as a gigantic wild Boar. We have reached the mammalian, quadruped form in the evolutionary ladder. The gigantic size continues to symbolise a conscious control of the genetic mechanism.

(4) **The Narasimha Avatara:** The myth has it that Vishnu next appeared as a monstrous half man—half lion apparition. We need not take this symbol too literally. The lion like mane and fierceness could well symbolise the Stone Age warrior or the early man. We have reached the evolutionary level of the biped primate, savage and strong.

(5) **The Vamana Avatara:** Vishnu appears as a grotesque, dwarf sized man—a Brahmin of exceptional intelligence. Does this mythical symbol represent the Ramapithicarus—the short sized humanoid that preceded the modern man?

(6) **The Parashurama Avatara:** The incarnation series reaches full human form with the sixth incarnation. Here we have Vishnu as a tall and fiery son of a Brahmin priest. The boy is renowned for his bouts of rage. This emotional clue is vital and will again be taken up later on for it could point to a stimulation of certain portions of the Limbic system that often occurs in the process of Kundalini arousal. In the historical setting of the myth Parashurama appears when the Kshatriyas or the ruling class are terrorising the populace. He takes up arms and faces the challenge from the social environment. In the process he proves to be a powerful military leader and great explorer who opens up new lands for Indo-Aryan settlement in the Indian sub continent. He engineered a social revolution that placed the states in the hands of the Brahmins (Intellectuals) rather than the warriors who had become oppressive and tyrannical.

**(7) The Rama and Krishna Avataras:** These are the most famous of the Vishnu Avatara series. The legends of Rama and Krishna have left a powerful and indelible impression not only upon the consciousness of South Asia but also upon that of all South East Asia itself. The Ballad of Rama is still celebrated in Java, Bali and Kampuchea. The Ramayana and the Mahabharata, which record these two lives, are amongst the greatest epics of the world. What is the historical veracity of these legends? Has all of South East Asia been held in thrall by a mere fairy tale with no basis in historical fact? The Rama Avatara is characterised by the lofty moral tone that he set. He was an exemplar for the Indian civilisation. He also proved to be a great military leader who defeated the King of Lanka and spread Aryan influence South of the Vindhyas. The Krishna Avatara is the most popular of this series. He is some sort of an Indian God Pan. A very charismatic and creative leader, he is a great synthesiser. He is the author of the Gita—one of the greatest scriptures of Hinduism that attempts a synthesis of all existing Indian schools of philosophy and yoga. He is also a great general who propagates the indirect approach in an Indian military environment that idolises chivalry and the direct approach. Krishna is a great statesman and diplomat—in short a man of action and deep reflection. The metaphor of the milkmaids who run after him with their girdles flying, serves to symbolise his tremendous charisma. Krishna serves as the role model of his age. He has a deep sense of history and a breadth of vision, which enables him to view with equanimity—the rise and fall of peoples and empires—including his own. Krishna is the archetypal, Indian Animus like figure—the combination of the sage who meditates, the seer who reflects upon the nature of things and the statesman and general who guides the course of human destiny. A many faceted and charismatic personality; a great communicator whose message and whose doctrine of desire-less action reach out across the centuries to influence the lives of the Indian people even in our age. They were the exemplars and revivalists of the Indian civilisation. Incidentally both Rama and Krishna conform to Plato's ideal of the philosopher king.

(8) **The Buddha:** The Buddha is the 9th and the last known incarnation of Vishnu. In the Buddha at last we have a historical personality that we can clearly identify. He has as yet not passed away wholly into legend and myths. The millions of Buddha icons proclaim to us the powerful personality of the Shakya Muni—the Enlightened one—the Light of Asia, whose message of Universal peace and harmony was far in advance of his age. The Buddha reflected deeply upon the ills of the present human condition. He exhibited a tremendous charisma that still holds people in thrall even 2000 years after his death. His tremendous diagnostic and communication abilities marked him out as a great prophet. He spoke and his resonant voice travelled over all of Asia—to China, Tibet, Mongolia, and the Central Asian Khanates to Japan, Korea, South East Asia, Burma and Sri Lanka. *The triumph of the Buddha represents a triumph of the Indian civilisation. The Indian civilisation abstained from physical conquest. It relied instead upon an ideological conquest of hearts and minds— a "Dharma Vijay".* Today when we stand in reverence before the serene and tranquil icons of the Buddha—we can only imagine the powerful charisma of that historical personage that reaches out across the centuries.

*Had Christ been born in India without doubt he would have been added to this list of evolved Prophets or Avataras.* He more than qualifies by virtue of his boundless charisma and his communication and diagnostic abilities. The historical personalities of these exalted personages reach out beyond the ravages of the centuries as powerful beacon lights. The Buddhas, the Christs and Mohammads indeed are the lights of this earth. Their influence upon the lives of men even in this age of impeccable, secular credentials remains overwhelming. It is here suggested that the release of the latent genetic potentials threw up these super charismatic entities, these civilisational icons and exemplars, these ideologues who spread their ideologies across the continents and ages.

**The Kalki Avatara:** The Puranic lore speaks of a tenth incarnation of Vishnu that is yet to come. Predictions have it that he will appear as a great warrior who will destroy the present industrial order (the Second Wave). He will end the present Kaliyuga or machine age, and usher in a new ecological age of harmony and growth. The Buddhist mythology speaks of the Maitreya Buddha—the Buddha who is yet to come. The Shia Muslims speak of a Shahi Buz Aman—a prophet who is yet to come.

Religion may well be the opium of the people but a neurosis that seems to afflict 99% percent of humanity does call into question our concepts of normalcy. It is time that science took a dispassionate look at religion. Does the effervescence of religion represent the fulfilment or vague yearnings and gropings for an evolutionary end? Different cultures in different geographical settings have given varied local expression perhaps to the same deep-seated human impulses. A yearning for understanding—a desire to interpret the universe in one unitary frame of understanding—a yearning for truth and beauty, harmony and light; for peace and bliss and understanding. The Vedas, the Zend-Avesta or the Bible or the Koran seek to provide the mind map of reality with which their followers can navigate through the vicissitudes of their individual lives.

However, going beyond these theoretical and ideological constructs, current research in America and Europe is clearly highlighting the fact that biologically, the human brain is hardwired for such mystical and religious experience. Most of the mystical phenomena are being traced back to their biological origins in the human brain. The ecstasy and the experience of incredible wideness can all be traced back to this biological basis. In fact Shamanism represents the first mystical upsurge in all primitive tribal societies. It has been called the cult of ecstasy. There is a strange commonality in Shamanic rites, practices and experiences in regions as far a field as Central Asia, North and South America, Africa and South East Asia. These primitive shamanic upsurges of the neuro-biological drive for mystical experience later evolved into the great world religions with all their complex ideologies and their source books. Most Shamanist rites involve a temporary withdrawal into solitude. Such withdrawals for "tapas" or "sadhana" are a part of the yogic lore. Most psychosomatic exercises to raise the Kundalini are done in the solitude of forest retreats. The lives of the prophets of the Middle East also record such withdrawals into solitude—into caves or on top of mountains to receive wisdom and hear the inner voices.

All great world religions are ideologies even as Marxism or Capitalism are ideologies. Erich Hoefer's "true believer" is on the march everywhere. The recent worldwide upsurge of religious fundamentalist revivals is proof of the strength of this phenomenon. The imperial strength of this powerful and primitive human urge for transcendence seems to defy our scientific attitudes. We must recognise its existence and its strength and seek to unravel its basis.

## Religion as Ideology

The myths and legends of the Indian civilisation are woven not around its empire builders but its Avataras and Bodhisattvas and its "evolved" beings. These were beings with their Kundalinis fully aroused. The Indians have been accused of having no sense of history. Yet the preservation of the utterances of the primal Vedic seers is an unparalleled feat of racial memory. For over two thousand years, thousands upon thousands of verses of the Vedas were committed to memory and passed on from father to son. The Vedas were finally committed to writing a few centuries before the birth of Christ. They are available in extant form even today—almost 5000 years after they were first composed: The Puranic folk lore records the lives of the Avataras—the incarnate beings who had undergone this process of evolutionary metamorphosis in their consciousness. It was supposedly a process that bestowed upon them the marvellous gifts of ecstasy, creativity and charisma and the archaic rhythms of poetry with its rhymes, meters and alliteration, enabled them to reach past the conscious censors and contact the collective unconscious of their people. *Obviously then the emphasis of the Indian civilisation was not on its empire builders and conquerors but on its mystics and ideologues.* The ideologues, who spun out the mind maps of reality with which their people navigated through the course of their existence. Why should we give any scientific credence to these myths and folk tales? The epics may have literary and aesthetic value but how can we ascribe any scientific basis to these myths? The Avataras and Bodhisattvas and the Prophets are largely figures whose historical veracity is often open to question. The kernel of fact has been so heavily overlaid with myth and exaggeration that it is difficult to sift the truth. What makes this phenomenon worthy of investigation however is the fact that these prophets or Buddhas or Avataric phenomena are not the only recorded incidents of such human transformations. *There are a large number of lesser-known cases of such "arousals" or biological transformations, which are scientifically even more important transformations than the Avatara series.*

This is because the stories of their lives have as yet not been embellished with gross exaggeration, and poetic metaphors. In trying to convert a human being into a mythical figure that will ever stalk the collective racial memory—the ancient propagandists had intuitively turned to exaggerations, embellishments, poetic licence and miraculous tales. They showed an intuitive grasp of the art of myth building. Subsequent Communist and Fascist ideologues and propagandists have tried to convert Lenin, Mao and Hitler into living legends in their own lifetimes. We have clearly been able to see the propagandist tools of exaggeration, distortion and amplification in action. Therefore, we cannot possibly lend much historical credence to the Prophet, Avataric or Bodhisattavic biographies. It is the lesser arousals that have not been overlaid with heavy drapings of embellishment and exaggeration that are of vital concern to us, simply because the truth is relatively easier to extract from these tales.

The severe trials and tribulations—the ecstasies and despairs and the inner summits of triumph of these beings form poignant tales in themselves. Creative people have generally been associated with the arts and crafts and even the sciences. Religious activity is also an intensely creative activity, for the religious person attempts to create a holistic and all encompassing overview that will explain the alpha and omega of his existence. He tries to fashion a personalised unified field theory as it were, that will provide a doctrinal overview for each and every facet of human activity and link it in a unitary frame of understanding. Each religion is an ideology. Each religious leader tries to create a master mind-map of reality. He theorises about the origin and creation of the universe—upon social relationships, customs, mores, rituals, and traditions. He tries to tie every aspect of human life in a unitary framework of understanding. Religious activity apparently is a Right brain lobe function of synthesis. It is a holistic activity of the human mind that tries to integrate human experience into one single and simplified ideological frame of understanding. The Bible, the Koran the Vedas or the Dhammapada are vast source book of an all-encompassing ideology. They seek to lay down for their followers their cosmological, social, political, economic and cultural beliefs. *It is time that we learnt to view religions as ideologies. It is time that we learnt to view religion as the inherent activ-*

*ity of the Right Brain hemisphere that constantly seeks to unite human experience in a unitary frame of understanding;* in a generalists overview that synthesises all the diverse disciplines and sciences. Religious activity represents attempts at fusion and synthesis. True, this impulse can often degenerate into genocide, murder, mayhem and worse but so can the powerful sexual instinct degenerate into rape, perversions, and sickness. We will be able to take a more scientific view of this religious phenomena if we learn to view it as ideological activity aimed at providing an holistic overview—a simplified guide map to synthesise all aspects of human experience a universal guideline for all true believers, monks and followers.

The religious person therefore is inherently an ideologue—a generalist who seeks to knit all aspects of human experiences into one single ideological frame of understanding. His deep convictions can (and often do) easily degenerate into fanaticism and rank intolerance. The same is true of all "true believers"—whether Marxist, Fascists or, Zionists or warriors of the Holy Jihad being waged by the party of God!!

Perhaps the intense revival of religious fundamentalism in the world today represents a worldwide upsurge of right brain dominant tendencies in the human race. The Third Wave will probably witness a rise in right brain dominance over left. Hence the search for unitary frames of understanding, for all embracing ideologies, which were first attempted by the religious prophets or the Avataras, Bodhisattvas and later by the Communists, the Fascists, Socialists and Nationalists leaders of all shades. These are all a right brain lobe function.

*The intensely religious person then is essentially an ideologue. He is also an intensely creative individual in whom the urge for fusion and synthesis is paramount. He is a person in whom the Right Brain lobe is the predominant mode of consciousness.* If we wish to unravel the mechanism of human creativity we must look deeply into the lives not only of the poets and painters and the sculptors and writers but also into lives of the mystics, saints and seers. And on the borderline lie the visionaries and babblers, the lunatics and madmen who all form grades of the same creative class. Neuro-theology has fast become a new buzzword among researchers. Modern Scientists have now clearly identified the Biological mechanism that predisposes mankind to mysticism, to religions fervour experience and ecstasy. The human brain is as hard wired for religions experience as it is for sex.

# CHAPTER FIVE

## KUNDALINI PATHOLOGY: CORRELATES OF THE CREATIVE PROCESS

### The Pathology of Creativity

In recent times *clinical studies of creative people (poets, artists, sculptors etc.,) have highlighted episodic work spurts and seasonal patterns of creativity. There are mood swings that are often accompanied by heightened energy, decreased need of sleep, grandiosity and euphoria.* These are often followed by moods of depression. This cyclothymiacs cycle appears to be the chief psychological motif of all creative activity. In its morbid states it leads to altering cycles of mania and depression.

Several verses in the Vedas mythologize such inner struggles in the form of myths. One myth is about the lost herds of Dawn. It is a deeply allegorical and mystical myth. In essence it depicts the onset of a newborn consciousness. The first visitations of the "Go" the inner rays or luminosities (Go incidentally means both cow and ray of light in Sanskrit). These are stolen by the Panis—the reptiles! These have to be relocated and rescued. One has to battle with the entities of the Dark side of the Force. It is a heroic struggle to regain the light to rescue the radiances of our inner dawn. We have to struggle on till the onset of the inner sunrise. The Atman, the psychic entity is described as the warrior, the eternal pilgrim, and the traveller to the truth. His inner struggles are as heroic as our external wars.

Van Gogh's "lust for life"—his lyrical creative transports and his stark, suicidal depressions are part of legend today. Sigmund Freud's "Grand Passions of the Mind" point to such intense struggles in the inner landscape. All creative art appears to belong to the domain of abnormal psychology: hence its linkage with madness, cyclothymia, mania, depression and even schizophrenia.

Similar mood swings between euphoria and ecstasy and morbid depressions have been recorded in the lives of many religious saints and mystics. St. Theresa's "wound of love" and the "dark night of the soul" are part of the pathology of mysticism. Indian folklore records a number of such biographical accounts. Some of the better-known ones are of the lives of Shankara, Ramanuja, Madhavacharya, Chaitanya, Raman Maharishi and Rama Krishna. We get a mass of clinical information on the emotional and physiological upheavals caused in their lives by their mystic practices. But easily one of the best-known accounts is the most recent autobiographical exercise of the Late Pandit (Pt.) Gopi Krishna. His is a marvellous account of inner transformation that has been recorded with clinical objectivity and deep humility. It provides a mass of physiological details and clinical data about the symptoms encountered in this creative pathology. It is an invaluable human document and may one day serve to build a bridge between subjective mysticism and the objective methods of science. It is a unique and unparalleled account of an odyssey into the inner landscape—a journey to the core of human consciousness.

Gopi Krishna had a core mystical experience of the so-called "arousal of the Kundalini" at the age of 34. For two decades thereafter he was seized helplessly by a relentless inner process of transformation. It was not merely a subjective process but was accompanied by severe physiological and psychological changes.

Gopi Krishna kept a detailed and clinical record of the changes that he witnessed in himself. His account therefore provides us a unique data bank on the clinical symptoms that are encountered in this creative pathology. It is this data that makes a scientific analysis of this Kundalini process highly worthwhile. What were these changes or symptoms? Based upon the account of Pt. Gopi Krishna and the accounts of earlier mystics (notably Ramakrishna) we can classify them under two heads as the physiological and psychological correlates of this creative process.

## Physiological Correlates: The Kundalini Pathology

This peculiar train of inner events is almost in all cases unleashed by *a core mystical experience*. The core mystical experience occurs in people who follow a reclusive life style. They are normally introverted personalities. Sometimes they consciously follow a yogic course of psychosomatic exercises to include contemplation, concentration and meditation. *In psychological terms it implies a lifestyle characterised by a cyclical as opposed to a linear view of time*. It often involves psychological processes that entail exercises of "directed attention" or concentration. It is a long drawn process that normally spreads over a few decades (though exceptional cases of rapid "arousals" are also on record). Very often there may be no conscious attempt at any esoteric type of concentration or meditation exercises. A reclusive or introverted life style and a degree of isolation are the only essentials. As a mystic said—"one has experienced it on the vastness of the sea, another in the majestic grandeur of the mountains and yet another in the endless stretches of golden desert sands". In some others this process has been triggered off by the humming sound of bees. The triggering may be sudden but the preparation process is generally long and drawn out. The vast majority of Eastern mystics have followed a definite set of psychosomatic exercises prescribed in yogic texts. These set exercises of concentration and meditation produce altered states of consciousness. These have recently been verified by EEG (electro encephalograph) measurement of Brain Wave Patterns (R. Keith Wallace and Benson: Experiments on TM subjects). They seem to initiate a new state of consciousness characterised by "restful awareness" and a marked onset of the alpha brain wave rhythm. Years of such practices sometimes yield the core mystical experience, which curiously seems to have common characteristics in many religions and cultures and especially the Eastern religions of Hinduism and Buddhism and superficially in the Sufi mysticism of Islam. The core mystical experience therefore merits elaboration.

## The Core Mystical Experience

*The core mystical experience has been characterised by a feeling of intense ecstasy, and an incredible widening of the consciousness. The point of awareness or the "I" within seems to expand till it gives a feeling of encompassing the whole universe. It is an oceanic feeling* of cosmic consciousness accompanied by intense rapture and ecstasy. It is a depth phenomenon that leaves an indelible stamp upon the entire subsequent life of the individual. It has an intense existential quality of "is-ness", an overwhelming reality before which all other reality seems insubstantial and hazy. It has mostly been described as an inexpressible experience of overwhelming rapture and beatitude. An experience that creates a revolution in the human consciousness and forever alters the "inner instrument" of the viewer. It is supposed to lead to trans-human states of evolved consciousness. It is often accompanied by experiences of intense light and radiance and roaring sounds within. This experience has been variously called the experience of "Nirvana", or "Moksha", or "Kaivalya", or "Liberation". In Indian philosophy it is described by the term "Sat-Chit-Ananda: Truth—Consciousness—Ecstasy". Indian mystics undergoing this core experience have verbalised it with the famous expostulation of "Aham Brahmasmi"—"I am Brahma"—an emphatic assertion of an oceanic feeling, a feeling of incredible expansion of consciousness that seems to encompass the entire universe in its sweep. In Sufi mystic lore it is characterised by "An Al Haq". In Buddhist lore this is called the experience of the great Void or the Shunyata. In Vedic terminology "the mind soars to those dizzy heights of grandeur—then falls like a wounded bird— what really shall I speak? What shall I think?" This Rig Vedic verse best captures that sense of awe, majesty and wonder that this experience arouses. It has variously been called the stage of Samadhi in yogic texts and Satori in Zen writings. What is more important from the research point of view however is the train of physiological changes that this core mystical experience seems to trigger off. It seems to be an autonomous/pre-wired programme as it were. The experiencer is supposed to "surrender" himself to this process, to abstain from any attempts at conscious control— to be merely a witness to the self—regulating process of change. This state of passivity has been extolled in mystic literature of various religions as surrender to the will of the "Divine". What is important to note is *that it does not appear as a trial and error process but as a teleological process that unfolds as a pre-wired programme of definite genetic and metabolic changes.* In most Eastern cultures (and especially in the great world religions of Hinduism and Buddhism) *these intense self-induced transports of ecstasy become an end in themselves.* They were intense and searing depth phenomena that shook the experiencer to the core of his being. They had an intense existential quality that made them unforgettable. They spawned a new cult of ecstasy. *The Eastern mystics had discovered new pleasure centres deep within the human brain.* They had discovered a new super orgiastic experience of Samadhi that almost occurred with the intensity of an inner super nova of rapture and beatitude. Where the culture of the West has run in thrall of orgasms that occur at the terminal end of the spine—the Eastern mystics opted for the super orgiastic experiences of the brain, hence the assertion that the greatest tactile rewards lay not in the world without but deep in the depths of our own consciousness. Hence the reclusive and contemplative lifestyles and attitudes of introversion that are common to Eastern religions. Having analysed and verbalised (to the extent possible) the "inexpressible" core-mystical correlates, let us turn to some of the other physiological and psychological changes induced. Pt. Gopi Krishna and others have recorded some of the following characteristics: —

1) Sessions of meditation caused a rush of blood to the head. *This caused a rhythmic rocking or swaying motion of the body.* Experiments conducted on meditating subjects with Ballistio-Cardiograms have recorded the onset of a standing wave in the Aorta. This spreads to the entire brain cortex (Issac Bentov experiments).

2) *A marked stability of posture occurs in the later stages of meditational practices. There is a total loss of the awareness of surroundings and the passage of time.* The eyes feel as if glued together and have to be forced open with deliberate effort after prolonged meditation.

3) Rise of body temperatures along the spine.

4) *Experiences of shivers or jerks up the spine in the early stages. Experiences of "goose flesh"* all over the back, the chest and the forearms. Coldness and lifeless feelings in the lower limbs.

5) Sudden and intense erotic arousals accompanied by tumescence and vivid erotic imagery.

6) Pressure upon the visual or auditory centres in the cortex seems to trigger off the experience of intense internalised lights and sounds phenomena. Sometimes a bright blue or red dot is perceived (with closed eyes) constantly for long periods. Visions of flashes of lightening and other visual experiences of-

ten culminate in the experience of perceiving a vast and unlimited ocean of light as it were. It has poetically been described as being brighter than a thousand suns. Pressure upon the tympanic membrane or the auditory cortex seems to trigger off the experience of internalised sounds variously described as the "hum of bees". The "roaring of a water fall" the "chirpings of insects" the "blowing of conches", or the "roll of thunder".

7) An acute state of metabolic disturbance. Ravenous bouts of hunger in which the experiencer could consume amazing quantities of food, followed by an intense aversion for the sight of food itself. Gopi Krishna also records an aversion to medication that is usually recorded in such pathologies.

8) Experiences of intense burning sensation within the body as if it was set alight by an internal fire. In the later stages it is marked by a feeling of indifference to external heat and cold. This relationship with temperature control is the most significant clue to the nature of the process. This suggests the intense involvement of the hypothalamus in the entire process.

## Psychological Correlates

1) EEG experiments on TM subjects in meditation have recorded the onset of a fourth stage of consciousness as distinct from waking, dreaming and deep sleep. It is characterised by what R. Keith Wallace and Benson have called Restful Awareness induced by a marked predominance of the Alpha brain wave patterns in the brain. The TM practitioners do not speak of the Kundalini. However, the meditational techniques practised by them are adaptations from the classical texts and are for all purposes the same as those employed by the practitioners of Kundalini yoga. The marginal differences lie in the choice of mantras or the focus sounds for meditation.

2) Cyclothymic Rhythms: The core mystical experience is usu- ally followed by the *onset of a cyclothymic cycle in the experiencing consciousness*. Pt. Gopi Krishna has described it as a "waxing and waning of consciousness". After the in- tense inner arousals, after the joyous and ecstatic peaks of the experience of trans-human consciousness, come states of stark depression and despair. In the wake of his mystical ex- perience. Pt. Gopi Krishna experienced a major relapse. He felt a revulsion for all forms of religious experience.

He gave up meditational practices and lived in a state of dread and horror. The state he describes easily fits the description of a manic depressive condition. This is substantiated in many mystic biographies (notably those of Christian mystics like St. Theresa). *Many other mystics have described this alternation in con- sciousness, these stark mood swings between ecstasy and depression. These mood swings seem to have a close and inti- mate linkage with the seasonal cycles.* It is as if some deeper biorhythms get amplified by a sudden release of energy from within the core of the psyche. The experience is quite akin to the sea- sonal affective disorder experienced by individuals in cold regions where in mood swings occur with the changing seasons. The core mystical experience occurs like a controlled "chain reaction" in the reactor of human consciousness. There are innumerable in- stances of this process occurring as an uncontrolled explosion as it were, an internal supernova that seems to disintegrate the core of human consciousness into confused and shattered fragments. It has led in the past to Schizophrenic states. Schizophrenia does seem to occur like an internalised explosion that rends the per- sonality of the victim into confused and shattered fragments. Pt. Gopi Krishna himself had pointed out to the similarities between the release of the Kundalini process and its possible derailment into the chaos of Schizophrenia. In others in whom this release of "energy"remains controlled and orderly, the cyclothymic cycle seems to get hooked (or plugged) into the larger climatic cycle of the seasons. *Mania and depression are the mirror images of this cyclothymic cycle.* The spring season is usually linked with the manic phase of this cyclothymic cycle. *It is characterised by heightened energy, reduced need for sleep, euphoric and ecstatic states of consciousness, increased creative activity, grandiosity and extreme states of religious fervour.* The same episodic work spurts and euphoric moods have been noted in the lives of creative artists and writers. The sine curve of inner energy then plunges downhill. In the hot summer and monsoon months it often slips into states of inner exhaustion and depression—a deep low in the individuals creative and emotional energies.

The physiological basis for these cyclothymic swings in the inner energy patterns may have a lot to do with collective "firing of the brain neurons and their refractory periods of neural exhaustion". These refractory periods could well coincide with the states of depression. This will be taken up in detail in the next chapter. It has been recorded in many mystic lives that this cyclothymic cycle has lasted a number of years till the typical sine curve of energy output levelled off—the neurons were strengthened as it were to sustain a heightened general release of metabolic energies without relapsing into refractory periods of blockage and exhaustion.

**Emotional Arousals**

Hyper arousals of emotions (or affective disturbances) have been recorded in the lives of many mystics. Fits of rage, irritability and irascibility have been noted in the lives of most creative persons. In the mystic, however, these seem to reach pathological proportions. The Bible records the travails of Job or the essential man. He rails against his fate and reviles his maker. His intense anguish has been expressed in the most lyrical and moving portion of the Bible. The lives of many Eastern mystics record such experiences of intense spiritual anguish. It is sometimes characterised by fits of weeping and evident emotional disturbance. In the Indian Yogic lore these fits of spiritual anguish are called "Bhavas". They are recorded in the lives of Chaitanya and Ramakrishna. Ramakrishna especially used to relapse into fits of agonised weeping in which his frame was convulsed with uncontrollable sobbing. St. Theresa has described such bouts of spiritual anguish as "the wound of love". Chaitanya, the mystic of the middle ages was a brilliant scholar. He was also very irritable and often experienced uncontrollable fits of rage. In his later life he used to go into emotional transports accompanied by outbursts of weeping. Indian mythology abounds in stories of sages who were prone to relapsing into sudden fits of towering rage. The Parashurama Avatara—the sixth incarnation of Vishnu is especially renowned for such celebrated temper. These emotional disturbances are mostly encountered in the early stages of the personal evolution of most mystics and sages. In their later lives (and especially after the core mystical experience has stabilized), they seem to slip into moods of tranquillity and great equanimity. There appears to be a definite process of emotional evolution that leads us from the self assertive class of emotions like lust, greed, avarice and anger into what Arthur Koestler has called the self-transcending class of emotions. These emotions are characterised by an expansion of feeling that transcends the boundaries of the personal ego. These include awe, and wonder, compassion and courage and ecstasy. The compassion of the Bodhisattvas extends even to the non-human forms of life—to every sentient creature on this planet—to the animal and plant kingdoms alike. The Vedic verses abound in such compassionate references to the good of all living beings. The boundless love of Christ or the compassion of the Buddha are manifestations of this class of self-transcending emotions. Altruism, charity, empathy and compassion all belong to this self-transcending class. So do the emotions of awe and wonder: the wonder of the scientist contemplating the majesty and grandeur of the universe, the awe of the cosmologist contemplating the big bang. Courage and fearlessness also belong to this self-transcending category of emotions that take a man beyond the confines of normal body consciousness. It is this, which gives the religious fanatic fighting for Jihad and holy wars his phenomenal courage. The emotional disturbances generated in the initial stages of this personal evolution, however, provide us a very vital clue to the physiological basis of this process. The Limbic system and the hypothalamus are the reptilian cores of our brains. These are basically the seats of our emotions. In laboratory experiments conducted on rats, electrical stimulation of various points in their limbic system produced intense reactions of rage or lust or fear. Certain pleasure centres have also been discovered in the limbic system of rats. These when stimulated initiated experiences of intense pleasure in these rats. In experiments electrodes were connected to external switches, which the rats could operate. Once the rats learnt the connection between the pressing of the switch and the onset of intense pleasure in their brains—they "blew their minds" as it were. Mindless of hunger and thirst or sex or any other distracting stimuli—the rats continued to press these pleasure switches till they fainted with sheer exhaustion.

Such experiments have since been replicated in human beings. Electrical stimulation of certain points in man's limbic system, have been known to elicit violent emotional reactions of rage or grief or anger and even ecstasy. Do the meditational processes involved in mystic practices then serve to stimulate man's limbic system? That alone can account for these paroxysms of rage or irritability, these bouts of intense anguish and weeping, these feats of bravado and inhuman courage, and its extreme these intense transports of ecstasy and rapture.

What is being played upon is the grand orchestra of the limbic system of mankind. The Limbic system in fact resembles the Harp musical instrument in shape. Its bio-electrical stimulation seems to trigger off our emotional transports along the entire range of human emotions; the affective spectrum that encompasses grief, rage, lust, bravery, fear, horror, humour indifference and ecstasy. The Indian literary tradition records them as the nine elixirs (Rasas) of human experience. The Kundalini process therefore seems to involve intense stimulation of the Limbic and Hypothalamic core of our brains and leads to these emotional upheavals and affective responses encountered in mystic biographies. The Hypothalamus is also responsible for our internal temperature control or thermostasis. These experiences of intense "heat" or burning etc., that are encountered in the Kundalini pathology could well be explained in terms of hyper activity of the hypothalamus. The hypothalamus is active even in the growth period of children. Babies tend to suddenly develop very high body temperatures in fevers. There is a Tibetan School of Yoga, which trains its adherents to acquire a conscious control of man's temperature regulating mechanisms.

These Tibetan Yogis have been credited with feats of sitting naked on ice and drying up to seven sheets dipped in ice-cold water with their body heat (Tumo) alone. There is a very close linkage between the body heat regulation and emotional mechanisms. Both are strongly stirred in the Kundalini process. Since these are the reptilian core structures of the human brain the references to the Kundalini as the "Serpent energy" are most apt and strikingly accurate.

The Hypothalamus acts as a sea-saw, an either-or mechanism in our psyches; a sort of OR gate in our bio-circuits. It has a very important role to play in the initialisation of our metabolic processes. The process of puberty incidentally is triggered off by signals released by the Hypothalamus. *So should be process of the Second Birth, which the Kundalini arousal entrains.*

**The Upsurge of Creativity.** Almost *all mystics have been without exception intensely creative persons. Most of them have left behind a prodigious output of religious literature.* They have either written or inspired vast amounts of spiritual literature that has been held in profound reverence as holy books of their race. The Hindu Vedas are the inspired verses of a number of mystics called "Rishis" or "Seers". The Dhammapada records the teachings of the great Buddha, the Bible records the teachings of Christ; and the Koran the teachings of Mohammad and the Zend Avesta ("Thus spoke Zarathushtra") are masterpieces of creative writing. In our times Vivekanand, the gifted disciple of Ramakrishna turned out an impressive volume of philosophical literature based upon his mentor's teachings. Aurobindo—the revolutionary mystic of Bengal has left behind an awesome amount of creative and inspired philosophical writing. The most recent such example is Gopi Krishna. He was a man with no intellectual background or university degrees to boast of—and yet he has left behind a profound autobiographical record of his Kundalini experience. His creative output has been prodigious in amount and most inspiring in content. His later inclinations to express himself in the archaic rhythms of poetry and rhyme specifically highlight the creative aspects of this phenomenon. *Classical poetry has an innate feeling for the primitive and archaic rhythms of man's consciousness. The rhyme schemes and meter symbolise the ancient tom-toms in primitive man's consciousness.* The rhyme schemes and archaic rhythms of primitive poetry appeal to the large unconscious portions of our minds. They serve to get past our conscious censors and appeal to the deeper levels of our unconscious selves. *The rhythms of poetry make it easier for us to memorise the verses and aphorisms of the mystic masters. The songs of the Sufi saints, the poems of Meera and the couplets of Kabir, Rahim and the Sikh Gurus are all enshrined in the archaic rhythms of pristine poetry.* In our age of reason and total recall based upon computerised memories, we have begun to neglect the rhythmic tools of poetry, which have served to keep alive our religious and cultural traditions. There is more to poetry than mere alliteration of sounds, the repetitiveness of rhymes and the literary artefacts of metaphors and similes. These are the ancient rhythms of the human mind—the sources of synchrony and resonance. *All inspired speech; all revelations have been expressed in these archaic rhythms and symmetries of language.*

Pandit Gopi Krishna in his later creative phases felt compelled to express himself in poetic rhythms. He wrote poetry not only in the English language but also in German of which he had no knowledge. True, the literary value of these poems may not have been very high but they highlight the expression mechanisms that utilise the primitive rhythms of sound and speech for appealing to the subconscious sectors of our minds. These expression mechanisms somehow become active after the release of the creative energy in the cores of our brains—the so-called serpent energy focussed from the reptilian cores of our brain structures.

**Freedom from the Linear View of Time.** Maha Kala in the Eastern Tantric tradition represents the relentless and destructive nature of time. It is the curse of our linear sequential mode of viewing Reality. *We perceive time as an inexorable one-way street that stretches from the Future to the Present and slips irreversibly in to the past.* Time is pictured as a terrifying monster into whose relentless jaws everything disappears into oblivion. He swallows up all that exists. Everything that is born must die. Decay and entropy seem to be the essential nature of things. "All constructions end in destruction, all acquisitions in dispersions, all meetings in partings"—the Buddha had grasped the inexorable nature of time as a great destroyer more than twenty centuries ago. But time is a relative phenomenon. *We can bring about a* *revolution in our worldview only if we can alter our perception of time. The Eastern mystical traditions sought precisely to free us from the excruciating fetters of a rigid and linear view of time.* From an obsessive concern with its fleeting aspects into a cyclical and tranquil mode of viewing reality developed a view of time not obsessed with its unstoppable, unidirectional flow into oblivion but a view that stressed the "is-ness"—that extended the fleeting moment into an eternity of bliss. Mahakali—the dark mother of the Universe represents the Entropic energy that can help us to destroy our deeply entrenched linear view of time. This relentless linear-sequential mode represents the tyranny of time. Carlos Castaneda had re-learnt what the Upanishadic seers had discovered many thousands of years ago. *We are conditioned from our birth into an acceptance of the consensus reality. Our reality is taught to us through the medium of our day-to-day experience. We must learn to unlearn our reality—to de-condition our minds of these imposed paradigms.* We can then proceed to learn newer modes of reality, which are perhaps the results of altered states of consciousness. And *the chief operant conditioning or limiting factor is our linear and sequential view of time.* The tyranny of time is the most overwhelming agency that conditions our minds to conform to a consensus reality. A freedom from the fetters of time alone can set us free. A release from the linear—sequential mode of viewing time brings about the onset of great tranquillity and equanimity. It is chiefly responsible for reducing stress and setting us free for creative pursuits. The greatest curse of Industrialism has been the vice like tyranny of its work schedules, time tables and factory production runs, its stark awareness of the fleeting nature of linear time. *We have let the mournful hoot of the factory hooter hypnotise us into accepting a depressing view of reality—into an artificial and mechanistic life style hopelessly divorced from the ecological (organic) and harmonious modes of living.* Stress is the greatest killer of our modern age. Stress is the chief product of our inexorable linear view of time as a one-way street... "A street without joy"— a street that stretches remorselessly from birth to decay and death and oblivion.

The Upanishadic cry for redemption echoes across the aeons.

"Lead me from darkness to Light.
Lead me from Untruth to Truth.
Lead me from death to immortality"

It is a cry for our redemption from the tyranny of time, from the fetters of a linear mode of viewing reality that has been imposed upon us by constant cultural conditioning. Such a view of time is the greatest enemy of the creative process. It is the chief affliction of mankind. It is the greatest source of stress. Mahakala, the monster of time is the great destroyer. Mahakali is the creative energy that sets us free from the fetters of a linear view of time. It appears therefore that a release of the inner creative energy seems to create a revolution in our perception of time. It erases the deeply entrenched racial programming for time measurements in our psyches. It liberates us from the linear modes of viewing reality and leads us into circular modes of time that generate tranquillity, peace and harmony. Leisure and creativity form a self-reinforcing feed back loop. The one leads to the other.

Most monastic orders and disciplines, very consciously seek to alter our concepts of time measurement from a linear to a cyclical mode. Some prefer to call this the process of "de-automation" a deliberate programme to de-condition our minds of this tyranny of a linear—sequential mode of time perception. Thus monks in the distant monasteries seek to follow routines and disciplines that are very repetitive and similar. Early morning meditation sessions, joint chanting in the Chaityas or Viharas, reading aloud from the same texts followed by more joint meditations and repetitive chanting of Mantras or Sutras. *The difference between one day and the next fades slowly. Our concepts of time in the monasteries, Viharas and Ashrams become cyclical instead of linear. They get plugged in to the rhythms of nature*—to the swing of the eco-cycles and bio–rhythms. These lead to happiness, de-stressing and ultimately to a revolution in the depths of psyches— A revolution called "Nirvana". The lives of most prophets record such a withdrawal into solitude that serves to lower the influx of sensory inputs that seems to release us from the fetters and flow of time.

# CHAPTER SIX

## KALA AGNI: THE VEDIC CONCEPT OF THE KUNDALINI

Time has an overwhelming directional momentum. It is forever speeding relentlessly from the Past to the Present and into a future that we do not know. So remorseless and overwhelming is its flow that it sweeps aside all forms and structures with its entropic energy. It swallows up civilizations and empires. It destroys all that we create, it causes all constructions to run down and become ruins that get buried by the sands of time. It is inexorable and relentless. It is the greatest destroyer. No wonder it is called Maha Kala—the monster of time that swallows up everything in its jaws. Such a relentless forward or directional momentum must flow from a great source of primal energy—the energy that powers the flow of time. Is this just a destructive and entropic power or does it also have a creative function? The energy of time fuels that relentless forward momentum of the inexorable flow of time. Mahakali, in the Indian system of philosophy is said to be the energy of Time that is at once entropic and destructive and creative and organising.

Time is a one-way street. In normal circumstances it can flow only in one relentless direction. When we make vortices of form in the river of space and time; we need to expend some energy to cause an obstruction to its flow, to create a vortex that will form a whirlpool in its flow. The form of the whirlpool remains constant even as the water in it is ever flowing and continually changing. Are all life forms vortices and whirlpools in the river of time? Can we tap the infinite energy inherent in the relentless momentum and flow of time?

The Vedas do not speak of the Kundalini. Very interestingly, however, they speak of the "Kala Agni"—the "Fire of time" or the energy of time. Agni and Soma, in fact are the two meta concepts of the Vedic Physics—even as Yin and Yang are the central concepts of Chinese philosophy. This dualism runs like a theme song through many diverse schools of Eastern philosophy— Shiva–Shakti, Chit-Shakti, Purusha–Prakriti, Yin-Yang, Akasha-Prana, and Agni–Soma etc. The concept of Kala Agni is most interesting and intriguing. The Energy of time that forms the vortex of the whirlpool of our life forms, is released and kinetised. It rises and as it rises, a revolution occurs in the depth of our psyche. The relentless arrow of time in us is reversed dramatically. The direction of the arrow of time is reversed in a manner that is revolutionary.

The biological organism is no longer pushed by its evolutionary past. It is no longer pushed by the evolutionary momentum of its past mutations. It is no longer guided by the digital information stored in its genes. The arrow of time reverses its direction. It is now pulled by its future evolutionary potentials. Morphic resonance now takes place in a radically different manner. Not the momentum of past evolutionary experience but the pull of the future now moulds the shape of the organism. It becomes a prophetic life form—no longer pushed by its past but pulled by its future morphogenetic potential.

The future shape steps back quantum mechanically to guide the unfolding of the existing form to its future potential. Morphic resonance now takes place in a dramatically reversed form. Not the past but the future exerts its guiding influence. Is it possible for the arrow of time to be reversed so dramatically? Nobel prize winning scientists like Ilya Prigogrine have theorised that it should be possible to reverse the arrow of time. Why should its flow be possible only in one direction, from the past to the present and into the future? Why can this flow not be reversed? Why can't the future flow backwards to guide the unfolding of the present?

The Vedas say it is possible. The Kala Agni rises. The flames of time rise. The prolonged processes of meditation entrain a revolution in our habitual and deeply ingrained perception of time (as a one-way street without joy). Apart from the imperial strength of its Entropic flow, we now experience its creative aspect as the direction of its flow is reversed dramatically. Kala Agni—the energy of time rises in our beings like a flame. The Soma descends in response. It bathes our beings in a deluge of ecstasy and euphoria. We feel ecstatic and lyrical. We experience grandiosity, mood elevation, heightened energy, euphoria ecstasy and a marked upsurge of creativity. The entropic flow of time is reversed. Our life spans are lengthened; the next stage in our evolutionary process takes over. The new evolved consciousness is characterised by the onset of ecstasy, positivity, brain wave synchrony, great release of inner energy, incredible creativity, charisma and enhancement of communication skills.

Such an evolved being, such a Prophetic life form focussed upon the future is called a "Kala Purusha"—a being of time. He is prophetic. He can sense the future. He can anticipate events. He becomes a visionary. He consciously leads the people towards the unfolding of their future potential. In Vedic times such a being was called a seer. He was a "Drashta" (Seer) of the sacred verses, of patterned speech, which gave insights into diverse fields of knowledge. Their utterances were stored carefully by families of sages and recorded for posterity as the Vedas.

Here in this dual process of an ascent of the Kala Agni and a descent of Soma we have a curious synthesis of the Tantric concept of the Kundalini that rises and the Aurobindan concept of the Super Mind that descends (to guide our evolution).

The process is best explained diagrammatically by the two inverted triangles that penetrate one another. This is the famous Sri Yantra cosmogram. The dot in the centre represents the Atman or psychic being. The rising triangle symbolises the Kala Agni. The descending triangle symbolises the Soma.

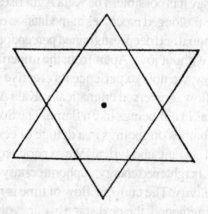

These two parallel processes serve to explain the intrinsic process of our psychic evolution in energic terms. Curiously, modern neurobiology tells us that the Frontal lobe of the brain deals with our time perception and is also the seat of our creative abilities. Meditation causes an upsurge in the reptilian cores of our brains—an upsurge that rises; and affects the frontal lobe in a dramatic fashion. It seems to entrain a train of pre-wired genetic potentialities.

Starting from the most primitive Shaman, the more evolved beings of this race felt compelled to retire to the solitude of a cave or a forest. There the rate of sensory input was markedly slowed down. In later yoga techniques this retreat was formalised and ritualised. The process of meditation further served to inhibit and reduce external stimuli and led the meditator to focus on his own consciousness. In those solitary retreats a quiet revolution seemed to occur in the frontal lobes of the human brain that measure time. Something happened to man's time perception that created a revolution in his psyche as it were. The prophets and sages who went into the great silence of the solitude came back radically transformed—ready to lead their flocks into a new future. The arrow of time had been reversed in their beings. Something in them had changed so profoundly and silently. Kala Agni—the energy of time had been kinetised. It had arisen and its rise entrained the release of some remarkable gifts of the great silence.

# CHAPTER SEVEN

## SOMA: THE NEURO TRANSMITTERS OF NIRVANA

### On Soma—The Diffused Elixir of Ecstasy

The Tantric view of the Kundalini was rather explicit. It blatantly identified it with our sexuality. It sharply localised this energy at the base of the cerebro-spinal axon. Tantric physiology charted out a complex structure of the human morphogenetic field. It elaborated in detail the three main Nadis or energy channels of the Sushumna, the Ida and Pingala and 72000 other minor nadis. It elaborated in detail upon the complex structures of the "chakras" or the Information energy transfer centres along the cerebro spinal axon.

The Vedas predate the Tantras. No mention of the Kundalini is found in the Vedas. However, the Vedas (as mentioned earlier) revered the creative energy within and addressed it in the Gayatri Mantra (hymn) as the Sun within, a subconscious but powerful symbol of the human libido. *The Vedic conception of this creative energy and its action were rather diffused and not so strongly localised as in the Tantric tradition.*

*The most beautiful sections of the Rig Veda are devoted to Soma. Soma is a marvellous concept.* Soma was supposedly a psychotropic elixir that conferred a marvellous ecstasy upon those who experienced it. It sparked off phenomenal creativity that expressed itself in the rhythms of beautiful poetry. Soma also conferred phenomenal courage and fearlessness upon the Aryan warrior. It made him drunk with power as it were; he felt grandiosity and euphoria and such a complete absence of fear that no foe could withstand him on the battlefield. The Vedic seers go into raptures over the wondrous and magical qualities of the divine potion of "Soma". *"It is the essence of the Sunlight, it partakes of the golden radiance of Hari the Sun"*. "It is equally the essence of the cold silver moonlight. It drips from the disc of the moon and bathes us in the soothing dew of the fulgent moon light". "Soma, the gift of incredible ecstasy: *Soma that moves the tongue to song". The incredible fire-bursts of Soma fill our minds with radiance and majesty, with awe and wonder.* "His power is clothed in the fire-bursts of the Sun". "His bellows bend our minds with power". The Soma Sukta portion of the Rig Veda that eulogises this incredible Soma is the most rhapsodical portion of the Vedas. Its songs are enshrined in the most marvellous and sublime poetry ever composed by man.

What indeed was this wondrous Soma? Was it alcohol? The idea is profane and vulgar. Gordon Wasson the German botanist says, *"It takes little perception to sense the difference between the awe inspired hymns to Soma and the rowdy drinking songs of the West prompted by alcohol"*. The Rig Vedic Aryans knew alcohol and called it Sura. Verses 86 of canto V11 of the Rig Veda highlight the difference between Soma and Sura. It says: "Malice has not been of my own free will, O Varuna, it was Sura, anger, dice and a muddled head".

Sura, the alcoholic potion left one muddle headed; it caused anger and malice. It could never serve as the inspiration for such marvellous and awe inspired poetry as one comes across in the Rig Veda. Soma was vastly different from alcohol. What was it then? Was it a psychotropic plant? *Gordon Wasson* thinks so. From the clues in the Rig Vedic hymns addressed to Soma he *has postulated that Soma was a psychotropic mushroom. He has identified it as the Amanita-Muscaria—the Fly Agaric mushroom of Central Asia.* It is a brilliant Red Mushroom with white flecks. The Shamanists of the Eurasian land mass have long known and used this mushroom plant. In his book "Soma the Divine Mushroom", Wasson has elaborated upon the poetic clues in Soma poetry to establish the identity of this psychotropic plant.

The clues are poetic and open-ended and could lend themselves to many interpretations. Many years ago I had the good fortune to meet a dedicated Botanist working at the Indian Forest Research Institute in Dehradun. In those days he was engrossed in an attempt to unveil the identity of the psychotropic Soma plant. He started with the same poetic clues as Wasson has used in his book. *Years of research based upon building a morphological description of the plant from the poetic clues in the Rig Vedic verses led him to identify it as a creeper plant found in the lower Himalayan slopes.* I vividly remember his jubilation and enthusiasm as he excitedly shared his discovery with me. Unfortunately KM Vaid, that dedicated Indian Botanist and researcher died before he could publish his discoveries of a lifetime of research. But the vision of his psychotropic plant have continued to haunt me ever since. Long after his death I could not shake off his obsessive concern for that plant that held the Rig Vedic civilization in such thrall.

Max Muller and Scheindler identified Soma as Sacrostemsa—a leafless bunch of green succulent branches with flowers like those of onion. However, in 1884 the British sent a commission to Afghanistan to determine its boundaries with Czarist Russia. One of its members was a botanist called James Edward Aitchson. Aitchson was trying to identify the Zorastrian Hoama (The Parsi equivalent of the Vedic Soma). He identified it as a species of Ephedra that grows in Afghanistan, Baluchistan, Kashmir and Western Tibet. The Ephedra is called Hum in Afghanistan. It comprises branches and sprigs, one mass of upright twigs. When covered with male flowers, the bush becomes golden in colour. This Ephedra yields an Alkaloid drug called Ephedrine. This simulates the nervous system and causes a general feeling of euphoria and heightened alertness. The debate continues. Soma in fact, is one of the last unsolved riddles of Indology. In the long years that followed I have thought deeply on this issue. I was also carrying out intense meditational practices under the guidance of my teacher. I had some remarkable experiences of that ecstasy that has been written about in the verses of Soma, the ecstasy that "moved the tongue to song", the ecstasy that filled one with awe and wonder. *The indescribable ecstasy that Professor James Old at Mc Gill University had succeeded in inducing in the rats in the laboratory by electrically stimulating the pleasure centres in their Hypothalamus!*

*It did not need the external agency of a psychotropic plant. It can be self-induced by the process of meditation. One can auto-stimulate these pleasure centres deep within the brain to experience the incredible tactile rewards of an inner ecstasy. For stimulation of these centres also leads to the secretion of endorphins and enkephalins, the opiates of the brain. These polypeptides lead to the experience of euphoria and mood elevation.* This euphoria eliminates the normal fear, panic, withdrawal and flight response to pain. The combat multiplier effect of such an attitude or mind set upon soldiers entering into battle can easily be imagined. It made the Indo–Aryan invincible in battle. It made him overcome his fear of death, wounds and darkness. He entered the battlefield in euphoric states of mood elevation that did not countenance the idea of defeat. Such a positive and fearless mind set is the precursor of victory. *Soma thus was the ecstatic eruption of neuro transmitters that sparkled in the human brain and "drugged" it into an incredible transport of ecstasy and bliss.* This transport produced a revolution in the lifestyles, attitudes and belief systems. To the soldier it gave incredible courage and a euphoric absence of fear and pain. *It was a self-induced drug, a naturally occurring opiate, a polypeptide that was not addictive, caused no withdrawal symptoms and that needed no external agency. It was produced directly by the human brain itself.* A Rig Vedic verse alludes to this phenomenon. It says: —

> They think they have tasted
> the true Soma when they
> crush the plants.
> Fools!
> The Soma, the true Soma.
> Only the Brahmins
> know that one".

The Rig Vedic civilization was carefully on the lookout for such beings who had mastered the art of auto—stimulation of these pleasure centres in the brain. For this stimulation led to a bountiful harvest of endorphins, dopamine neuro-transmitters and hormones. *These were the fuels of ecstasy, creativity and charisma. These were the main springs of a phenomenal accretion in verbal skills and communication abilities. The external signs of such a man were visible in his euphoric states of rapture and his creative intelligence, which expressed itself in marvellous poetry.* Thus Shuna Shepa—one of the Rig Vedic seers was called the *"Ananda Stambha"—the pillar of ecstasy (as stable in the state of ecstasy as a pillar).* He was also a "Mantra-Drashta"—a seer of the inspired verses. Poetry came effortlessly to him, not as a struggle with rhymes and metre schemes but in a holistic fashion, in a fully completed form. The sages, the Rishis or the wise ones recognised one another in the assemblies of the learned by the recitation of these holistic verses.

So the Rig Vedic Aryans consciously sought to promote the *introspective life styles and psychosomatic exercises that yielded such a rich harvest of hormones and endorphins. These are the biochemical fuels of creativity. The pastoral Indo Aryans then were engaged in an inner agricultural process that stimulated the neurons to yield the nuggets of the ecstasy inducing neuro-peptides.* For apart from ecstasy (which often became an END in itself), it led to the unfolding of a brilliant and creative intelligence. The gift of creative intelligence gives the community the gift of a creative minority of visionaries, thinkers and integrators. To its soldiers and men of action the gift of these endorphins gives euphoric states of mood elevation that overcome the fear of pain and death in battle.

This diffused "Somatic" concept of Soma as an eruption of neuro-transmitters in the brain gives us a radically different concept of the Kundalini—but one that could be far, far closer to the truth. Like Aurobindo's Super Mind, its action is largely confined to the transfer centre of the human brain and not the base of the cerebro-spinal axon.

Today we can recognise the psychotropic action of the mythical Soma plant in the form of the neuro-peptides (the endorphins) secreted by the human brain. Perhaps these peptides are also found in the plant world. They are not in the Fly Agaric Mushroom. Perhaps they are in the Himalayan creeper plant that Vaid had discovered or in the Ephedra bush. Who knows? The secret has died with that obscure Indian Botanist of the Forest Research Institute—a seer and a sage if I ever saw one.

## The Sacred Fire

The Vedic view of the Kundalini as Soma was far closer to the biochemical reality of the phenomena. The mystic fire was the most sacred symbol of the Indo–Aryans and the Iranians. Perhaps this fire in the altars was merely a symbol of the metabolic internal fire that consumed the food in the body and nourished our cells. Perhaps it was a symbol for the burning of glucose in our glial cells to supply the creative processes of the neurons in the human brain. The Soma was poured into this sacred fire as oblation. It fed the fire. So were the food and the clarified butter fed to this sacred metabolic fire that keeps our beings alive.

*The altered state of consciousness that Soma brought in its train was called "Rit Chit"—the Rit consciousness* or the bliss consciousness marked by stupendous levels of ecstasy and creative intelligence, by serenity, tranquillity and a harmonious ecological life style in total harmony with nature. To unfold this radically new concept let us first take a detailed look at Neuro-transmitters themselves. These are the true basis of the physiological action of the so-called Kundalini process. The nature of their action is much better explained by the Vedic concept of Soma. It is essential therefore to take a detailed look at the neuro-transmitters.

## The Neuro Transmitters of Nirvana

The Anti–Histamine drug Promethazine was used by neurosurgeons to calm patients as early as the 1940s. It led to the development of the wonder drug Chlorpromazine by two French psychiatrists (Jean Delay and Pierre Deniker). This drug calmed mentally ill patients (produced euphoric states of quietude) and between 1952-55 was found useful in the treatment of "schizophrenia". Subsequently Imipramine, a derivative was found useful in treating depressions. Lithium has been found useful in treating mania. *The development of these psycho active drugs led to an understanding of the processes that these drugs trigger in the brain of patients suffering from the psychotic disorder of schizophrenia, depression and mania.* This led to an explosion of research into the field of Neuro-transmitters.

## Neuro-Transmitters

*The brain is a vastly complex "super bio-computer". It is the crowning glory of human evolution.* In complexity and information storage and handling capabilities it is a marvellous instrument. Not only is it the basis of our linear, sequential logic, but also of holistic and creative thought and our moods, affects and the lyrical transports of complex emotions. It comprises mainly of two types of cells—*the neuron cells that conduct and transmit the electrochemical impulses of information and the Glial (or the Glue cells), which support, nourish and insulate the neurons. Glucose is burnt in these cells to provide the energy fuel for the working of this bio-computer. These glial cells far outnumber the neurons. The neurons however, are the wonder cells designed to communicate electro-chemically with one another.* Neurons, unlike other body cells cannot replace themselves by cell division. They thus lay the basis for the mortality of the human organisms. Each Neuron has three main parts: —

(a) **Cell Body.** This is a minute blob made up of the central nucleus and surrounded by cytoplasm. Nutrients and waste products keep filtering in and out of the permeable cell walls to keep the cell body alive.

(b) **The Axon.** This "Tree trunk" shaped axis transmits signals from the cell body to the other cells via the junction called synapses.

(c) **Dendrites.** (Like Trees) are net works of short fibres that branch out from an axon and synapse with the end of axons from other neurons. Dendrites are receivers that bring in signals to the neuron body.

## Ion Speak.

*How do neurons communicate with one another? Signals course through the brain and nervous system in a relay where electrical impulses alternate with chemical* messengers. The electrical impulses flow through the Axon—dendrite pathways. *Chemical messengers (the neuro-transmitters) leap the gaps (synapses) between the neuron axon and the dendrite of neighbouring neurons.*

What happens is something like this. Before an electrical impulse arrives an inactive neuron has more Potassium Ions (K⁻) than Sodium Ions (Na⁺). The opposite holds true outside the neurons (i.e., there are more positively charged Sodium ions than negative Potassium ions). *Thus the inside of the cell is kept negatively charged and the area outside the cell membrane is kept positively charged.* When an impulse reaches the axon tip of a neuron it yields Neuro-transmitters. These chemicals burst from tiny sacs in the buttons forming the ends of the axons. *These neuro-transmitters cross the narrow synaptic gap and lock on to the receptor sites in the target (or neighbouring) neurons membrane. This alters the permeability of the cell membrane and lets the negatively charged K (Potassium) ions flow out and the Sodium ions flow in.* It thus alters the charge inside the membrane. *This area of reversed charge is the nerve or electro-chemical impulse, which excites an identical charge in the area adjacent to it and go on all the way down the axon.* Once the impulse has passed the Sodium ions are pumped back out of the cell. *After a brief recovery period the original charged state (negative within, positive without) is restored and the axon is ready to conduct another impulse.*

| Na ⊕ | K ⊖ |
|-------|-----|
| Na ⊕ | K ⊖ |
| Na ⊕ | K ⊖ |
| Na ⊕ | K ⊖ |
| Na ⊕ | K ⊖ |
| Na ⊕ | K ⊖ |
| Na ⊕ | K ⊖ |
| Na ⊕ | K ⊖ |

Excitory and Inhibitory Neuro Transmitters.

There are therefore two basic types of neurotransmitters (NTs).

**(a) Excitory:** These make an electrical impulse flow through a neuron (examples are Acetylcholine and Noradrenalin) and hence are called Excitory neurotransmitters.

**(b) Inhibitory:** These types act to block electrical impulses through a neuron. Examples are GABA (in brains outer grey matter) and Glycine (in the spinal cord).

At any one instance a neuron may receive thousands of contradictory signals from other cells with which it is in contact. Whether or not it fires off an electrical impulse depends upon how many signals of each type it receives. Hence neurons really act like minute information processors and their selective work prevents mental chaos. As Electroencephalography shows the brain is always firing with electro-chemical activity. Yet it some how sorts out for "attention" only those signals that matter. It can do this because *a neuron's cell membrane can switch from negative to positive and back again in no more than one thousandth of a second and strongly stimulated neurons fire faster than others. Thus an excited neuron firing at 1000 firings per second stands out from the general background "noise" as a machine gun burst stands out distinctly from a background noise of rifle shots.*

## Classes of Neuro-Transmitters

*Over 120 different types of neuro-transmitters have been identified in the brain.* One general classification can be made on functional basis (i.e., excitory or inhibitory). However, neuro-transmitters can also be *classified on the basis of their chemical complexity and structure.* Based upon this system of classification we can divide all neuro-transmitters into three categories. These are: —

    (a) *Simple Amino Acid Neuro transmitters.*
    (b) *Mono-Amine Transmitters.*
    (c) *Peptides and Polypeptides.*

The simple Amino acid Neuro-transmitters are the most widespread and are found all over the brain. Their action is very generalised and constitutes the bulk of the signalling process in the brain. The Mono-Amine transmitters are more complex chemical structures and account for only about one percent of the signalling traffic of the brain. However, this seems to be a very vital percentage that is responsible for the major psychoses like schizophrenia and manic–depressive disorders. The major psychoactive brain drugs like Acetylcholine and Serotonin are based upon this class of neuro transmitters. The third category is the most complex class of neuro-transmitters. These are called the peptides. *Peptides are two or more amino acids chained together in head to tail links. (The largest peptides have 44 amino acids).* The first peptides were isolated from cattle brains and turned out to be the *signals that control the body's endocrine glands and salt and water balance. In this class have been discovered opiate like Peptides or* naturally secreted opiates of the brain, which act as pain killers and induce euphoria and ecstasy. These opiates are mainly of two types: —

(a) **Enkephalins:** These are opiatic peptides produced by the brains *limbic system* and counter act depression by promoting a *natural equivalent of the euphoria induced by opium derivatives.*

(b) **Endorphins:** These naturally occurring opiates are secreted by the *pituitary gland.* These peptides *also generate euphoria and help the body handle pain.* About two-dozen such peptide neuro-transmitters have been identified which help the body to cope with pain. *These neuro-peptides have been proposed as the bio-chemical equivalent of Soma— the "psychotropic elixir of the Gods".* These peptides and polypeptides are highly complex molecular messages and act in concert with their associated monoamines and amino acid neuro-transmitters. The ratio of peptides to monoamines and Amino acid neuro-transmitters are 1:100:10,000 (i.e., for every one peptide molecule there will be a 100 Mono-Amines and 10,000 Amino acid neurotransmitters found in the brain). Thus the peptides act as a triad (or a cascade) with their associated Monoamines and Amino acid transmitters. *Georges Unger of the Houston University has established that learning seemed to involve the formation of peptides in the brain. The pituitary, Para Thyroids and pancreas also produce hormones that are basically peptides.*

In the possible transfer of information from the Informational field to the body, the signalling seems to be initiated by these complex Neuro-transmitters. *The peptides and Polypeptides are the most complex bio-chemical messages that can be delivered from the field to the brain. These act upon the endocrine glands and serve as the basic signals that initiate all metabolic and hormonal activity.*

Some of the important neurotransmitters are listed in the classification chart.

## CLASSIFICATION OF IMPORTANT NEURO TRANSMITTERS

| Type of Neurotransmitters | Excitory | Inhibitory |
|---|---|---|
| Simple Amino Acids | Glutamate Asparate | Glycine GABA (Gama Aminobutric Acid) |
| Mono Amine Transmitters | Dopamine Excess causes schizophrenia Epinephrine Nor Epinephrine Lack of these causes depressions. Drugs that boost these counteract depression. Nor epinephrine also regulates appetite and blood pressure. | Acetylcholine Sero tonin Nor Adrenalin (these are both excitory and inhibitory) |
| Peptides and Polypeptides | Enkephalins Endorphins (natural opiates of the brain, pain killers, mood elevators, euphoric agents and also trigger signals for the endocrine glands.) | |

## Chemical Degradation

*In experiments it was found that longer lasting artificial peptides do damage. Cells seem to prefer their peptide messages in frequent intermittent deliveries (discontinuous deliveries).* (It is tempting to think that cells seem to need peptides in "*Quanta's*".) It was found that long lasting (acting) analogues of Luteinising Hormone releasing peptides (which regulate the secretions of gonadotropic hormones from the Pituitary glands) actually turned down the receptivity of the responsive cells. *Over use leads to a process of chemical degradation or desensitisation. This "Quantum dosage" principle seems to be the general rule in the neuro-physiological realm. Neurons after "firing" go into a refractory period" of recovery during which they cannot conduct.* This recovery period can be quite short (as less as the thousandth of a second) *but over-exposure to highly complex peptides neuro-transmitters can lead to a severe chemical degradation or desensitisation, which can have a reversed effect. This principle is very important in our model of the neuro-physiological basis of the action of the Kundalini.* This exhaustion theory could well explain the episodic work spurts in creative art and the manic-depression (cyclothymic) cycle in abnormal psychology.

To understand the action of Soma or Kundalini let us fall back to study the action of certain wonder psychoactive drugs that have become very popular today for treating psychoses: —

**(a) Chlorpromazine.** As stated this wonder drug was synthesised by two French psychiatrists (Jean Delay and Pierre Deniker) in 1950. *Chlorpromazine blocks dopamine and nor-adrenaline and causes a decrease in central sympathetic activity.* Now Dopamine is a vital neuro-transmitter that in excess leads to schizophrenia. Chlorpromazine was found to be very useful in the treatment of schizophrenia as it blocked the secretion of dopamine (or de sensitized its receptors). *Chlorpromazine also reduces libido in males by blocking dopamine action on the hypothalamus and pituitary glands.* Total blockage of Dopamine by using chlorpromazine, however, can lead to Parkinson's disease.

**(b)   Acetylcholine and Serotonin:** These drugs *boost the production of the mono-amine neuro-transmitters called Nor-epinephrine and Dopamine and help to counteract depression. Depression would therefore result from a fall in the levels of these monoamine neurotransmitters.* Imipramine, a derivative of chlorpromazine and MAO are also useful in counter acting depression. The Neuro-transmitter *Nor-epinephrine also regulates our appetite and blood pressure. Excessive production of this could cause ravenous bouts of hunger. Lack of this could lead to a revulsion for food. Both these symptoms are part of the Kundalini pathology.*

**(c)   Lithium Carbonate** was found useful in the treatment of Manic-depressive cycles of violent mood-swings. The exact nature of its action however is uncertain.

Soma: The Neuro-peptide Model of Kundalini Action

Let us briefly recapitulate some of the symptoms encountered in the Kundalini pathology and reinterpret them in the light of our knowledge of Neuro-transmitter and Hormonal secretions from the endocrine orchestra.

**(a)   A Core Mystical Experience** of an incredible expansion or widening of consciousness, accompanied by INTENSE Ecstasy and the perception of brilliant light (described as an ocean of light).

**(b) "A Waxing of and Waning of Consciousness"**—the onset of a manic depressive cycle; *violent and seasonal mood swings that alternate between phases of grandiosity and euphoria accompanied by heightened energy levels, intense creative activity or religious fervour, and reduced need for sleep. These are invariably followed by all pervasive moods of depression inner exhaustion*—a revulsion for any form of religious experience—a stark awareness of one's condition—a revulsion for food—a drying up of ones emotional well springs for warmth and affection.

**(c) Intense Increase in Metabolic Rates:** Perceived as an *intensification of the "inner fire"*, quick burning up of fuel. (In the manic phase PETT scans reveal that *the brain burns up enormous quantities of glucose*). These are accompanied by thorough and quick elimination of waste products from the body.

**(d) Hunger:** Metabolic disturbance seems to cause *ravenous bouts of hunger in* which the subject could consume enormous quantities of food. These are followed by phases in which the very sight of food appears sickening.

**(d) Burning Sensations:** The victim feels as if set alight by internal fire.

**(f) Emotional or Affective Disturbance**—Violent emotional or libidinal arousals. Violent fits of rage or anguish accompanied by fitful weeping.

**Correspondence Chart** To relate the pathological symptom with the underlying Neuro-physiological process let us tabulate these in a chart:

| Kundalini Pathology: Symptoms | Possible Neuro-physiological Basis |
| --- | --- |
| 1. Expansion of Consciousness | 1. Stimulation of Reticular formation in the brainstem; deprivation of Sensory input to Left Parietal lobe of the Brain. |
| 2. Intense Ecstasy | 2. Massive release of Peptides (Endorphins and Enkephalins) Natural opiates of the brain stimulation of pleasure centres in the Limbic system and Dorsal Hypothalamus. |
| 3. Intense Light—"Ocean" of light etc. | 3. Pressure on/stimulation of visual cortex. |
| 4. Manic Phase. Heightened energy creativity, grandosity, euphoria, reduced need for sleep, religious fervour, intensity, and enhanced drive. | 4. Massive release of endorphins and/or enkephalins type peptides and associated Monoamines to include Dopamine and Norepinephrine. |
| 5. Ravenous bouts of hunger | 5. Excessive production of Norepinephrine. Stimulation of ventro-medial Nucleus of the Hypothalamus. |
| 6. Burning Sensation | 6. Stimulation of Preoptic region of the Hypothalamus. |
| 7. Libidinal Arousals | 7. Action of Dopamine on Hypothalamus and Pituitary glands. Action of peptides (Lieutenising Hormone releasing peptides) on these glands releases gonadótropic hormones. |
| 8. Emotional Arousals | 8. Stimulation of the Limbic system, Hypocampus and Amygdala. |

The Kundalini Action then seems to be triggered by a lava like eruption of neuro-peptides in the brain along with their associated Monoamine transmitters especially Dopamine, Serotonin and Norepinephrine. These neuro-peptides—the Enkephalins erupt in the Limbic system and the Endorphins in the Pituitary gland. *The Hypothalamus seems to be the very core of this disturbance or metabolic supernova. This sudden and massive release of neuro-peptides seems to have a dramatic effect upon the Reticular formation—which is the seat of consciousness in the brain stem. Meditation process leads to a significant drop in sensory input to the Left Parietal lobe of the Brain. This seems to bring about an incredible feeling of an experience of widening of the consciousness.* It sets the endocrine orchestra clanging in a rousing crescendo. *Gonadotropic hormones flood the system and lead to powerful libidinal arousals.* The Thyro-tropic hormones fired off by the Pituitary activate the Thyroid gland and accelerates the body's metabolic rate. *The sudden rise in levels of Norepinephrine leads to violent bouts of hunger. Stimulation of the Preoptic region of the Hypothalamus, which deals with temperature control, could produce the burning sensations described in Kundalini Pathologies. Stimulation of the Limbic system could lead to violent rage or affective reactions and could explain the irascibility or hyper-emotional states—the feats of anguished weeping of the mystic pining for union with "God" or the "Divine" etc.* All these symptoms correspond to the mania phase—the sudden, sometimes violent release of informational energy. At the neuro-physiological level it leads to a veritable eruption, a supernova of neuro-peptides—the Endorphins and Enkephalins opiates of the brain along with their associated mono-amine transmitters (Dopamine and Norepinephrine) and the simple Amino acids. The metabolic rate is sharply accelerated. The brain burns up enormous quantities of glucose in its glial cells and the entire endocrine orchestra is set clanging.

## The Exhaustion Phase: Chemical Degradation

This violent release of informational energy in the form *of Soma—the Neuro-peptides of Nirvana—is bound to be followed by a process of neural exhaustion. Cells seem to prefer their peptide's messages in quanta's, in intermittent deliveries. A continuous release of peptides chemically degrades the receptor sites of the neurons and makes them insensitive (desensitizes them). This seems to activate a negative bio-feed-back loop. It leads to a steep drop in the level of:* —

(a) Neuro-peptides enendorphins and enkephalins — The ecstasy and mood elevation vanish.

(b) Norepinephrine and Dopamine — Leads to depression and exhaustion. Hunger goes down. Sight of food is repulsive.

(c) Gonadotropic Hormones Thyro Tropic Hormones — Reduced Libido Reduced metabolic Activity.

*The neurons of the brain inundated by this eruption of neuro-peptides* and their train of associated mono-amine transmitters and simple amino acid neuro-transmitters *seem to step into a collective refractory period which witnesses a sharp drop in the levels of these stimulating or* mood elevating neuro-transmitters. *We have the classical basis for the onset of the cyclothymic cycle—the onset of mania followed by depression.* The waxing and waning of consciousness—the episodic work spurts of creative people the violent mood swings between ecstasy and despair—The ecstasy of our endorphins—the ecstasy of Nirvana followed by the "dark night of the soul".

## Soma: the "Drink of the Gods"

*Soma then was the Vedic terminology for the effusive eruptions of neuro-peptides in the brain. The secretion of natural opiates like the endorphins and enkephalins, which generated euphoria and ecstasy and eliminated the normal fear, panic, withdrawal and flight response to pain. It made the sage and artist creative and brilliant in synthesis and learning. It made the warrior fearless in the field of battle. Drunk with his own endorphins he lost all fear of death.* No wonder the Indo-Aryans so highly prized Soma. No wonder it was the most divine psychotropic elixir of the Gods. No wonder the Rig Vedic seers inebriated themselves with ecstasy in extolling its divine virtues. *This psychotropic substance was a naturally produced opiate that unlike its external counterparts was not addictive or habit forming. It was not harmful to the brain and body. It was in fact the basis of mans evolution towards altered states of consciousness characterised by bliss, ecstasy, creativity and charisma—A* state of creative brilliance when the human intelligence scales new heights by Fusion and Synthesis. Fusion and Synthesis make the sun shine in all its brilliance. The human intelligence blazes forth in creative brilliance by the same creative processes of fusion and synthesis. Soma made the Vedic seers burst out into marvellous and inspired poetry. The same process of informational energy release mediated by the release of neuro-peptides-made Pandit Gopi Krishnan turn to the archaic rhythms of poetry. Creative synthesis has always been the hallmark of the illumined mind.

The initial massive release of energy comes in a rush that over a period of time chemically degrades the neuron receptor sites. This leads to a phase of neural exhaustion when the output of the neuro-transmitters plummets dangerously. Depression and exhaustion last till the neurons recuperate again to receive the second quanta of Endorphins and Bliss. Very often *this sinusoidal in-*

*flow of energy gets plugged into the rhythm of the seasons. In spring when the entire biosphere turns fertile and creative the human mind open itself to the bounty of the great Field.* The goodness, and bliss of the field descend in the human mind to teach him the joys of fusion. Spring the season of mid summer madness, of poets, lovers and madmen all fuelled by the inner fuels of the endorphins and hormones and enzymes.

*This is the basis of that Manic-Depressive cycle that characterises the domain of the creative mind. The episodic work spurts and seasonal mood swings, all gifts of that great and all encompassing field of Information and energy from which flow the neurotransmitters of Nirvana—the Soma elixir of Endorphins and Enkephalins.*

The model of the Vedic Aryans was thus far closer to the biochemical reality than the later versions of the Tantras that lost themselves in a maze of sensuality and libidinal expressions. Nevertheless both schools of thought hold glimmerings of the truth that underlines all existence. We have now reached a stage of scientific development where we can become starkly aware of the great Field. The Field or the Force of the Jedi of science fiction! *(The Field that envelops all living things and is the source of all intelligence, bliss and creativity.) The release of Soma or the Kundalini occurs from this Field and directly acts upon our brains to secrete a powerful flow of neurotransmitters; a triad of peptides, mono-amines and simple amino acids that bring such exalted elevations of mood—such experiences of euphoria and ecstasy.*

The mode of the release of energy may sometimes be too sudden and abrupt for the frail organism to bear. The very psyche could then disintegrate into the chaos of schizophrenia and the neurons could be overwhelmed by a supernova of Dopamine that rends the personality into incoherent fragments.

Alternatively the neurons could stand up to the flow at first and exult in ecstasy but soon prove weak and relapse into a manic depressive cycle till the gush or the flow either evens out or tapers off. The manic depressive phase may last a number of years.

In the organism that is really ready, that has been prepared by years of silent practice, the transformation may occur not as a sudden revolution but silently and painlessly. The person may not become aware of his own exalted state for months and years. But such a smooth transformation is rarely possible.

A Rig Vedic verse says: —

"He tastes not the delight

who is not ripe

whose body has not

been tempered

by the flames of that fire.

They alone can bear that joy.

They alone can enjoy

the rapture

who have been tempered

by the flame".

# CHAPTER EIGHT

## A HARVEST OF HORMONES: REFLECTIONS ON THE ENDOCRINE ORCHESTRA

### Paired Structures of Consciousness

*I*ndian Philosophical texts are replete with reference to the dualistic nature of consciousness. Consciousness has two complimentary aspects: the cognitive and the Energic. It is Chit-Shakti (Consciousness-Energy) or Chit-Agni. It is symbolised by the union of Shiva and Shakti. Many Tantric icons and Tibetan Thankhas depict Gods in sexual union with their female consorts or shaktis. This sexual union is perhaps the best motif for the symbiotic nature of these dual aspects of consciousness. In the Sankhya system (one of the six Indian Schools of philosophy) *this ultimate pair is expressed as Purusha and Prakriti.* (*Purusha;* The male being—the cognitive aspect: and *Prakriti;* Nature—the feminine or creative aspect). *The Yin-Yang theory of Taoist philosophy expresses the same dualistic aspect of consciousness, even more forcefully. Yang is masculine, linear, aggressive, rational and practical. Yin is feminine, intuitive, demure, gentle and receptive.* The Chinese monogram of Yin and Yang best symbolizes the symbiotic union of these aspects at all levels. *It is a curious fact of biology that all the structures that serve to express human consciousness are paired.* The human brain–the seat of human consciousness is divided into two distinct lobes or hemispheres joined together by the Corpus Colossum. As has already been elaborated in earlier chapters the two brain lobes serve to express two distinct modes of consciousness. *The Right lobe deals with holistic, intuitive functions using shapes and patterns in its thought processes while the left lobe deals with linear–sequential logic using words and numerals in its functioning.* The other physiological structures that have significant bearing upon our consciousness are the *glands of the endocrine system.* They secrete the hormones that not only trigger many important physiological functions but also have a great effect upon our moods and emotions. *In particular they govern our metabolism, our sexual drives, our aggression and flight-fight responses of fear and self-preservation.*

These ductless glands are eight in number. These include: —

(a) The Hypothalamus.
(b) The Pituitary Master Gland.
(c) The Pineal Gland.
(d) The Thyroid and Parathyroid in the Neck.
(e) The Thymus gland in the Chest.
(f) The Adrenals above the Kidneys.
(g) The Pancreas.
(h) The Ovaries (in females) and Testes (in males).

Each of these glands will be studied in detail subsequently. But *the interesting fact is that all these glands (except the pineal) are paired structures. Collectively they constitute a highly efficient orchestra that governs the metabolism and functioning of the human body. The Pituitary, Para-thyroids and Pancreas produce hormones that are basically proteins and peptides in chemical terms. The Thyroid and Adrenal glands produce hormones that are either aromatic compounds or steroids (complex substances made of interlocking rings of carbon compounds). Together they constitute an information system of awesome complexity. All the hormones that they produce are borne in the blood stream. It is only the Medulla of the Adrenal gland that is triggered directly by the sympathetic nervous system to secrete Adrenaline and Noradrenaline that are central to mediating the crucial "flight-fight" response in the body.* These glands will be studied in detail a little later but the fact that must be highlighted at this stage is the paired nature of all these information structures in our biochemical information system.

*The endocrine system works through a series of negative feedback loops* (much like a thermostat used for central heating). *The negative feedback loop principle is also used in the guidance of missiles but they are used only once and the complexities of action they can be made to perform are quite limited. The endocrine orchestra is vastly more complex in its management of information.* It is important to study *these glands* in greater detail *for they correspond in location to the seven chakras mentioned in Kundalini texts.* Various tantric and yogic texts have differed in their description of the number and nature of these chakras or centres of energy. To some they represent the seven mythical planes of consciousness. Each chakra represents the point at which that plane of consciousness interacts with the human body. The ancient tantric symbolism was a complex conjecture about the space-time geometry of human consciousness. The symbolism dwelt in great detail upon the structure of each chakra. In shape most of these represented lotuses with varying number of petals. Each had its presiding God and his Shakti or moving energy. Most important *each chakra had a "seed mantra" or basic acoustic note that corresponded to it. Constant sub vocal repetition of this "mantra" or acous-*

*tic note was supposed to set up a kind of biological resonance that actuated the latent energies of this chakra.*

The chart below tabulates the chakra, its physical location and its so-called "seed mantra" or basic acoustic note.

| Chakra | Location | Mantra |
|---|---|---|
| 1  Sahsarara | Top of the Brain | Om |
| 2  Ajna | Between the eyebrows | Ham |
| 3  Vishuddhi | Base of throat | Ksham |
| 4  Anahata | Heart | Yam |
| 5  Manipur | Navel | Ram |
| 6  Swadisthana | Behind sex organs | Lam |
| 7  Mooldhara | At the base of the spine | Vam |

The Kundalini energy was supposed to be lying dormant (in two and a half coils) at the root or mooldhara chakra at the base of the spine. Tantric texts mentioned how it was to be aroused and taken up through the seven centres to the highest centre in the human brain. As it crossed each Chakra, it "opened" it. Most modern practitioners of Kundalini Yoga have laid varying degrees of emphasis upon these chakras. Pt. Gopi Krishna did not encounter or experience any "chakras" in the arousal process of the Kundalini. *My own teacher felt that the only chakras of consequence were those located in the brain—the lower chakras were merely the reflections or action centres of the higher chakras in the brain. There are various interpretations of these energy transfer centres. Most yogic scholars opine that these are not located in the physical body but in the psychic structures of consciousness—more specifically in the so-called energy body (pranayama kosha) and mind body (manomaya kosha).*

Modern physiology of course has found not the remotest signs of these chakras in the human body. However, *the correspondence of the sites of these so called chakras with the glands of the endocrine system and the nerve tissues is quite significant and has been noted earlier* in the book. Possibly this once again highlights the fact that the Kundalini motifs like Kekule's dream symbols are pictorial clues that indicate the underlying physiological mechanisms and have to be correctly interpreted in the light of physiological facts.

The symptoms encountered in the Kundalini pathology, to include violent disturbances in metabolic rates of the body, violent pangs of hunger or equally violent aversion for food, sudden experience of great thirst or violent libidinal arousals, all indicate a mobilization of the endocrine orchestra in this process. The endocrine orchestra and its effervescence of biochemical essences (the hormones) have a very significant role to play in the actualisation of our creative potentials. *It is possible that the ancient philosophers were referring to the glands of the endocrine orchestra when they spoke about the so-called chakras.*

The degree of emphasis on the "chakras" or endocrine glands would have to be studied in relation to the action of the Neurotransmitters in the brain. The bulk of the biochemical traffic occurs in the brain. Command signals and tropic hormones secreted there activate the lower endocrine glands. Hence the Vedas laid emphasis on the brain itself. The Tantras on the other hand delved deeper into the body and highlighted the action at the endocrine level. A closer look at the endocrine level glands therefore may help us to understand this biological creative mechanism in a better light.

## The Endocrine Glands

**The Hypothalamus:** The Hypothalamus and its extension, the Pituitary gland, constitute the core of the endocrine system. *All* *the trigger signals originate here. This is the central control and monitoring facility—more or less the Central Processing Unit (CPU) of the human bio-computer.* The *Hypothalamus acts as a "sea-saw" an either-or mechanism.* Most of the negative feedback loops with the other endocrine glands are controlled from here. *The two halves of the autonomic nervous system have their headquarters in the hypothalamus—the sympathetic system in the Posterior (or rear) Hypothalamus and the Parasympathetic in the Anterior (or frontal) hypothalamus.* The hypothalamus is a significant thermostat of the human body and is responsible for the preservation of the constancy of the internal environment. This it does by: —

(a) **Glucostasis.** The balance of the antagonism of Adrenalin and insulin.

(b) **Thermostasis.** Balance of the Vasodilatation and Vaso constriction *rear hypothalamus and sympathetic nervous system counteract cold by constricting blood vessels and increasing thermal output of the heart. The Anterior hypothalamus and parasympathetic system cool the body by vasodilatation.*

(c) **Emotional Homeostasis.** The same mammalian temperature control mechanisms come into play in the display of emotions. *The sympathetic nervous system mediates the rage response and the parasympathetic mediates the lust response.* The hypothalamus—the headquarters of both the autonomic nervous systems therefore serves to keep *the balance between lust and rage and therefore between the primary emotions of love and hate.* British researchers including Geoffrey Harris had as far back as 1965 *showed sexuality to be built into the hypothalamus.*

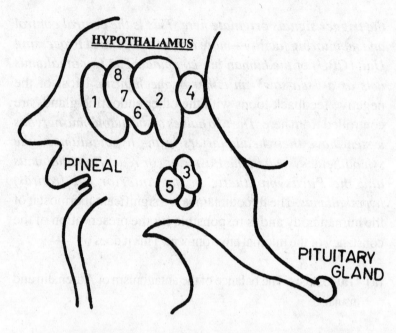

There are in fact seven hypothalamic regions each with a specific function: —

**(1) Posterior Hypothalamus.** Regulates sex drive and temperature control.

**(2) Anterior Hypothalamus.** Regulates water balance (and temperature control in conjunction with the posterior hypothalamus).

**(3) Supraoptic.** Also controls water balance.

**(4) Preoptic.** Also deals with heat control.

**(5) Ventromedial.** This ventromedial nucleus controls hunger.

**(6) Dorsomedial.** Controls aggression.

**(7) Dorsal.** Pleasure centre.

*The hypothalamus is no larger than the thumb tip and weighs only 14 gms., Yet this performs more tasks than any other brain structure of its size.* Its seven regions, as seen, between them *regulate body temperature,* control thirst and appetite, influence blood pressure, sexual behaviour, aggression, fear and sleep. It controls the pituitary gland and liases closely with the limbic system. Reinterpreting the Yogic symbol of the Sharsadhara charka—or the thousand petalled lotus—the entire brain with its million of neurons seems to act as the physical counterpart of this chakra. The hypothalamus however, seems to be the core of its "aliveness". Even physiologically this thalamic region (diencephalon) lies at the core of the brain. *It is suggested that the hypothalamus is the real seat of the Kundalini and not the sacral region.*

## Pituitary: The Master Gland

Behind the nose and between the eyes corresponding exactly in location to the classical "Ajna Chakra" is the *Pituitary Gland, the Master gland* or the so-called leader of Endocrine orchestra. The pituitary ("slime") gland owes its misleading name to an old notion that nasal secretion originated in this pea sized nerve centre. The pituitary is almost an appendage of the hypothalamus, which in fact controls the pituitary storage and output of hormones. The pituitary is basically two glands in one (as stated earlier this paired design is common to all information structures).

(a) **The Anterior Lobe:** This produces the *tropic hormones that control the activities of other endocrine glands.* (e.g. Thyrotropic hormone that controls the Thyroid gland; ACTH which controls the Adrenal glands; Gonadotropic hormones that stimulate the gonads to produce FSH (Follicle stimulating hormones) and LH (Luteinising Hormones). These control the production of testosterone and spermatozoa in the testes and the secretion of oestrogenes and progesterone in the ovary). In addition *it secretes the soma tropic growth hormone that controls the growth of the body.* Over secretion of this can lead to gigantism and under secretion to dwarfism. There is also a third hormone called lutetrophin. It has been discovered that ACTH and MSH hormones secreted by the pituitary *aid concentration.*

(b) **The Posterior Pituitary:** This stores hypothalamus-produced hormones regulating urine output and so helps conserve water in the body. It also influences oxzytrein production and the process of lactation.

## Pineal Gland: The Biological Clock

The Pineal Gland is a small red body, similar in shape to a pinecone and is situated near the corpus collosum. It projects down above the back of the brain stem and poses an enigma. *People once considered it a vestigial third eye. Nerve pathways to the eyes connect it and it shows surprising sensitivity to light.* New research suggests that it is *a light sensitive clock that affects sleep and other glands and seems to govern our biorhythms.* This seems to serve as the equivalent of the mythical "third eye" of the yogic tradition. It seems to govern our biorhythms. When darkness falls, the eyes indirectly inform the pineal gland, which then secretes melatonin—a hormone that effects brain cells that use serotonin. This is a sleep related neuro-chemical transmitter located in the reticular formation, the part of the brain responsible for consciousness.

## The Thyroid and Para-Thyroid Glands

This is situated at the base of the throat and corresponds in location to the classical "Vishudhi chakra". It consists of two lobes and is intimately connected with the metabolic activities regulating the chemistry of the tissues. *It controls the metabolic rate—when too much of this is produced the "fire of life" burns more fiercely and consumes great quantities of fuel.* This gland is activated by the Thyrotropic hormone produced by the pituitary and the levels of both are controlled in a negative feed back loop mechanism.

**The Para Thyroids:** There are four glands placed two on either side of the thyroid gland in the neck. These secrete para-thormone, which regulates calcium metabolism and controls the amount of calcium in the blood and bone.

## The Thymus Gland

This corresponds in location to the "Anahata Chakra" the heart centre. It is pinkish grey and consists of two lobes. Its functions are unclear. Recent research suggests that it *helps the body recognize and reject foreign substances* including bacteria and viruses. It secretes the THF Hormone (Thymic Humeral).

## The Adrenal Glands

These are situated on the upper pole of each kidney and may correspond to the Manipura chakra. They comprise of an outer yellowish part, the cortex and an inner portion called the modular.

(a) **The Cortex.** The Cortex is triggered by the ACTH hormone secreted by the pituitary gland. It produces *cortisol* (a close relation of cortisone), which *is a sugar-regulating hormone.* Excess of this would cause the *conversion of body protein into sugar.* It also produces the salt-regulating hormone. (This in excess would cause loss of potassium and retention of sodium and water in the system). In addition it also produces sex hormones.

(b) **The Modula:** *The modula is not triggered by blood borne hormones but directly by the sympathetic nervous system.*

This produces *adrenalin and non-adrenalin and is the Adrenal alarm system of the body that prepares it for the "flight–fight" response.* Non-adrenaline raises the blood pressure and Adrenal-Adrenaline aids carbohydrates metabolism by increasing the output of glucose from the liver. Location-wise this gland corresponds to the classical Manipura chakra. Interestingly enough in the yogic lore this centre was supposed to govern "aggression".

**The Pancreas:** Location-wise these would conform to the manipura chakra only. The islets of leagherthorm in the Pancreas secrete insulin. This controls the storage of sugar as glycogen in the liver and nerves as the body reservoir of energy.

**The Gonads:** These are the sex-hormone producing glands. They occur as ovaries in female and testes in males.

**(a) The Ovaries:** Produce oestrogenes and progesterone female sex hormones. The FSH hormones secreted by the pituitary stimulate the production of oestrogen provide for the development of female sex organs and secondary characteristics. The Luteinising Hormones (LH) secreted by the pituitary, control the production of Progesterone by the ovaries.

**(b) The Testes:** These secrete the male sex hormone testosterone under stimulation from the ICSH hormones secreted by the pituitary. This results in the development of male sex characteristics (beard, deep voice, enlargement of penis). The spermatozoa are formed in the testes.

The sexual gonads conform to the Swadishithan charka—the chakra that was incidentally supposed to govern sexual activity as per the yogic texts.

## Summary

*A detailed description of the endocrine glands and the hormones they secrete is essential to understand the actions of the Kundalini process* .For even a casual glance will show that *most of the symptoms encountered in Kundalini pathology, increase in metabolic rate, enormous increase in appetite, sensation of burning or an inner fire are all traceable to excessive hormonal secretion by the hypothalamus, pituitary and thyroid glands.*

Had *the ancient Indians discovered some means of stimulating the endocrine orchestra to hyper-activity? Had they discovered some acoustic sound structures, which caused bioresonance when repeated sub-vocally; a resonance that stimulated the endocrine glands to hyper-activity?* Or was it simply *"directed attention" focused on the site of these endocrine glands* that caused them to secrete the desired hormones in copious amounts? Indian Yogis of the Hatha yoga school have demonstrated *that man can acquire conscious control over a lot of involuntary bodily functions that take place at the autonomic level.* Some Indian yogis have demonstrated the ability to slow down their heartbeats, raise or lower blood pressure at will and even go into catatonic trances, which permit them to remain buried for days. They have acquired conscious control over visceral and glandular response. A conscious control of the endocrine orchestra—*an inner coup that overrides the functioning of its negative feed back loops and brings them in the domain of conscious control could literally perform miracles in man's consciousness. Such a control could give him an abundant harvest of desired hormones*—hormones that enhance his sexual, creative and charismatic capabilities—Hormones that enhance the aggression levels of the warrior and make him unbeatable and fearless in combat—Hormones that assist the creative writer, artist the scientist in his problem solving pursuits. *With a conscious control of our endocrine system, we can engage in a fascinating new form of inner agriculture.* We can reap a bountiful harvest of desired hormones.

# CHAPTER NINE

## THE NEURO BIOLOGY OF NIRVANA: THE EXPERIENCE OF GREAT WIDENESS

The core mystical experience in essence is a triad of inner experiences characterized by the Sanskrit term "Sat-Chit-Ananda". 'Sat', as stated earlier, stands for the overwhelming reality of the experience. The brain is the organ of perception. We perceive the world through it in terms of the disturbances or biochemical changes the external world causes in it. The core mystical experience occurs as an internal revolution in the organs of perception *per se*. As such it feels overwhelmingly real. It alters our organ of perception and reality itself. It is therefore experienced intensely as the ultimate reality. The next facet is the experience of a great widening or expansion of the consciousness. The point of "I" within seems to expand till it merges with the vastness of the cosmos itself. There is an overwhelming feeling of a dissolution of the boundaries of being and an infinite expansion of consciousness. The neuro-biological basis of this facet of the expansion of consciousness will be taken up in much greater detail in this chapter.

The Last two chapters had gone into the neuro-biological basis of the experience of ecstasy, mood elevation, heightened energy and euphoria. The neuro-biology of the Ananda aspect of the Nirvana experience has been covered at length.

A number of clinical studies of late have highlighted the fact that the human brain seems to be intrinsically "hardwired" for the experience of "mystical states". These seem to stem naturally from the neuro-biology of our brains per se. The recording of religious experience all through our history stems from this biological basis. The brain is structured to express various categories and levels of mystical experiences. This accounts for the widespread and almost universal nature of the religious experience. There is a commonality of structure in these religious/mystical experiences across all cultures. The core experiences have a surprising degree of commonality that transcends religious denomination and geographical boundaries.

## Shamanism

The earliest upsurge of religious feelings in all continents and cultures manifested as the primitive upsurge of Shamanism. Shamanism was the precursor to organized religion. It is still prevalent in many primitive, tribal societies and probably reflects a primal, human urge for transcendence. The fact that its basic tenets are so similar in diverse tribal cultures all over the world, clearly points to the biological basis of this phenomena. Human brains are as hard wired for the experience of religion as they are for the experience of sex. That explains the common features in Shamanism—the first manifestation of the human urge for transcendence and the later core mystical or peak experiences of the organised world religions.

Marcea Eliade, in her illuminating book "Shamanism: Archaic Techniques of Ecstasy" has in fact called Shamanism a technique for generating ecstasy. Shamanism, in the strictest sense is pre-eminently a religious phenomenon of Siberia and Central Asia. However, much the same underlying tenets and phenomena are encountered in the tribal lore of both North and South America, Africa, Australia and South East Asia. Many Shaman rituals of initiation entail the onset of ecstasy with the aid of "helping spirits". Ritual singing, dancing and monotonous beating of drums also puts the Shaman in altered states of consciousness that lead to the onset of ecstasy and visitations by human and animal spirit forms. The Shaman ritually goes into trances in which he can see or foretell the future or carry out ritual healing. Some of the most common Shaman rites are: —

(a) **The Shaman Retires to Solitude** in the mountains or caves where he stays alone for extended periods. He engages himself in ritual singing and dancing. He contemplates the sky. In the end he falls asleep and dreams of his animal or spirit helpers. The animal deities often help him to "learn their language" and enable him to foretell the future.

(b) **The Ascent:** A most interesting Shaman ceremony involves the cutting and planting of Birch Tree Poles. Ritual sacrifices are made here. As the culminating part of the initiation ceremony, the Shaman master and his pupils climb these Birch Poles and go into ecstasy. This completes their initiation. The ascent of the pole is an interesting rite—Possibly the external ascent triggers off the internal ascent of the psychosexual energies, of the Kala Agni or the Kundalini. The end result of ecstasy is common. In subsequent organized religions in the East, the withdrawal to solitude has been formalised in monastic orders that seek solitude and retreat to practice the psychosomatic exercises of concentration and meditation. An inversion of time is invariably involved by practices that lead to de-automation, and release from our habitual linear-sequential modes of perceiving time. Ritual chanting still forms a major part of most monastic disciplines. Ritual dancing is still practised by Sufi mystics and Dervishes in India and Iran.

The strange commonality of some Shamanistic practices in diverse tribal cultures—in Central Asia, Siberia, Europe, North and South America and amongst the aborigines of Australia and the tropical jungles of South East Asia and Africa—underline the biological basis of human religious experience. The human brain is intrinsically hardwired to undergo such experiences. They are an inherent part of its circuitry; hence the commonality of practices and experiences across diverse cultures and continents. Shamanism represents the earliest upsurge of religiosity and mystical/transcendental experience in primitive man. Many mystical practices in later organized world religions can be traced back to their roots in Shamanism—the retirement to solitude, ritual singing, chanting and dancing and beating of drums, trances and practises that lead to ecstasy and techniques that include the contemplation of the Blue sky and its sheer voidness of space.

## The Vedic Wideness of Being

The nascent seeds of spiritual and mystical experience are clearly visible in Shamanist practices. In the later mystical practices of Hinduism, Buddhism and Jainism these acquired very high levels of sophistry born of an insight into the underlying psychosomatic basis of these experiences. However, even in the sophistication of later practices we can clearly discern their roots in the Shamanist rituals and rites of primitive man in all their utter simplicity and profundity.

There are many Vedic verses that refer to the incredible widening of being. They allude to the experience of that incredible expansion of awareness and of ones being. The point of "I" within seems to expand in an infinite fashion till it is one with the cosmos. The Vedic expostulation "Aham Brahmasmi" (I am Brahman) or "*Soham*" (I am he) seems to sum up this experience of cosmic connectivity and an incredible wideness of being.

A Vedic verse describes it as the "Vast Light—the *Brihat Jyoti*". Another describes it as the "Vast Truth—the *Ritam Brihat*". A verse from the Rig Veda says: —

"The Dawns broke forth in their radiant splendour
Meditating, the Angirasas found the WIDE LIGHT.
Those who desire, open themselves to the
Wideness of these lights.
And the waters for them flow from heaven.

(R.V. VII. 90.4)

Other Vedic verses talk of that wide world—the Uruloka—
"a world of *vast light* and *wide freedom* from fear".

The incredible expansion of being, the dissolution of our ego
boundaries leads to that experience of merger with Brahman.

## The Neuro Biology of Nirvana

**The Experience of Wideness:** The brains of humans seem to
be hard wired for the experience of God. Andrew Newberg of
the University of Pennsylvania propounded the biological theory
of religion. He is a leading figure in the new and emerging science
of "Neuro-theology"—which explains the links between spirituality
and the brain. Newberg's theory is based on research begun in
the 1970s by the late Eugene D' Acquli, a psychiatrist and
anthropologist. D' Aquili's theory described how the brain could
explain a wide range of religious experience. In the 1990s D'
Acquli teamed up with Newberg—a radiologist. They refined his
theory and began testing it using an imaging technique called
SPECT (Single Photon Emission Computed Tomography)
scanning. They scanned the brains of meditating Buddhist monks
and Nuns (injected with radioactive IV)—especially at the time
of the peak experience. The scans photographed blood flows,
indicating levels of neural activity in various portions of the brain.
Their findings were thought provoking. The brain's left Parietal
lobes is the orientation—association area. The region is responsible
for drawing the line between the physical self and the rest of

existence—a task; that requires a constant stream of neural signals and information flowing in from the senses. The scans revealed that at the peak moments of meditation, the flow to the left parietal lobe was dramatically reduced. As the orientation area was deprived of the information needed to draw the line between the self and the world—the scientist believed the subject would experience a sense of limitless awareness—melting into infinite space, into an incredible WIDENESS of being!

Zen and the Brain: In his path-breaking book (Zen and the Brain) on the subject of neuro-theology, Dr James Austin of the Massachusetts Institute of Technology has done a very comprehensive study of this subject that is remarkable for its wealth of insights. Dr Austin had personally had a peak experience of a sense of enlightenment and oneness with the universe. He experienced a sense of eternity. He analysed this experience in very great detail and unravelled its Neuro-biological underpinnings. In order to feel that time, fear and self-consciousness had dissolved, he identified the following brain circuits that would have to be dampened down or suppressed: —

- Amygdala: This monitors threats and ignites fear. It would have to be suppressed to feel that experience of utter fearlessness. (This Amygdala incidentally, is the brain structure that causes you to jump instinctively when some one cries, "snake". It bypasses the cortical passage totally. It is an inheritance from our stone age past of fear and terror).
- Parietal Lobe: This circuit orients you in time and space; and marks the sharp distinction between the self and the world. These must go quiet or be deactivated and toned down. The greater the toning down, the more the feeling of wideness and incredible expansion—the melting of the boundaries of being.
- Frontal and Temporal Lobe: These circuits mark time and generate self-awareness. The threading of life experience on

the linear axis of time is done by the frontal lobe. This circuit must be disengaged.

"Spiritual experiences are so consistent across cultures, across time and across faiths", says David Wolff, "that it suggests a common core that is most likely a reflection of the structures and processes in the human brain".

In mystical experiences, the content of the mind fades, sensory experience drops out, and so you are left only with pure consciousness. Meditation restricts sensory inputs to the brain, helps trigger off these mystical experiences by reducing inputs to the specific brain region and structures. *People with a propensity for spiritual experiences are usually very creative and innovative, with a breadth of interests and great tolerance for ambiguity.* However, brain imaging studies have shown that even non-spiritual people can be moved to religious, experience by religious ceremonies and liturgy—drumming, dancing, incantations, all rivet attention to a single intense source of sensory stimulation and at the same time evoke powerful emotional responses. These sensory stimulations cause the Hippocampus (the area of the brain structure that maintains equilibrium) to act like a traffic cop and inhibit the flow of signals between neurons. This causes the religious neuro circuit areas to be deprived of the neural input and possibly leads to some of the mystical experiences referred to in this chapter.

The important point to note is that today Neuro Scientists have unravelled the biological basis of most of our mystical experiences. The human brain is hardwired for such experiences. The "circuits of God" seem to be a part of our racial inheritance.

The first upsurge of religiosity in ancient tribal cultures expressed itself as Shamanism. There is a strange uniformity of practises and experiences in Shamanism that is global. The subsequent world religions evolved from this early Shamanist upsurge.

They grew more sophisticated and elaborate in form, content and ritual practises. On the surface one sees a great deal of differences. However, deeper analysis indicates a surprising degree of commonality in the core teachings of various world religions. The human brain has some intrinsic "God circuits". These are taken over and programmed by the Shamans, with doctors, prophets and priests. Possibly in the decades to come, a synthesis of science and religious dogma will lead to a new, sophisticated version of Shamanism based upon the universality of consciousness and an understanding of depth ecology.

# CHAPTER TEN

# THE TREE ARCHITECTURE OF THE MIND: SILICON VERSUS HYDROCARBON INTELLIGENCE

## The Brain as a Bio-computer

The third wave is the crest of the electronic revolution. Quite possibly it is a false crest. For beyond the booming technology of silicon-based artificial intelligence and the burgeoning computer culture, is the revolutionary technology of genetic engineering or biotechnology. It is this that will be the mainstay of the third wave civilization. It will lead man back from his paradigm of artificial production and the resultant soulless machine age metaphor into a more organic culture that once again glorifies "growth" and a more participative and ecological outlook. It is precisely this outlook that will bring us back in harmony with nature.

Dr. Robert Jaston and other messiahs of the electronic revolution have prophesised that "a new era of silicon based life, indestructible, immortal, infinitely expendable is beginning. There is no limit to the rising curve of silicon intelligence". In a world where information was being generated at an astronomical rate, at a rate that threatened to blow the fuse of the conventional information storage and handling devices available with mankind, the computer was a logical and necessary development. Without it, the species would have blown their information fuse as a result of sheer overload. Computers based on silicon chips have given a total recall capability to mankind. This has multiplied his information storage capabilities a thousand fold. The ability to handle ever-larger amounts of information leads to a far richer and more stimulating environment. All this has been made possible by computers and the rising wave of silicon intelligence.

But *the computer enthusiasts and the media may have blown the electronic revolution out of all proportion. The new miracle of silicon intelligence is blinding us to the far greater miracle of Hydrocarbon based intelligence. An intelligence based not on metallic silicon chips but on colloidal hydrocarbon based chips of the DNA and RNA.* These hydrocarbon-based chips are remarkably robust. They can survive in extremes of climate and privations, they can live through war and mayhem; they do not need a clinical dust free environment like the silicon chips. *Their greatest miracle is their ability to replicate themselves.* This makes them so cheaply and so abundantly available that we have blinded ourselves to the miracle of the super-intelligence that they represent. *It is only when man tries to duplicate this intelligence by artificial means that he realises the true miracle of hydrocarbon-based intelligence.* It represents a superlative order of intelligence that is so well harmonized with the ecology of our biosphere. Its replication is facilitated by the rewards of sexual ecstasy. This makes it so cheap to mass-produce that it is threatening to deluge the world with its sheer physical creativity. *Sadly, the ease and cheapness of its "Production" detracts from our reverence for this form of intelligence.*

The media overkill deludes us into thinking that silicon intelligence is vastly superior to the antiquated intelligence of the colloidal Hydrocarbon chips—the neurons. We forget the staggering superiority of hydrocarbon intelligence over the Artificial

| SILICON (AI) | HYDROCARBON INTELLIGENCE |
|---|---|
| (COMPUTER) | (HUMAN BRAIN) |
| 1. Deductive Reasoning | Inductive and Deductive Reason |
| 2. Non-Perceptive | Perceptive |
| 3. Non-Creative | Creative |
| 4. No emotions | Complex Emotional Abilities |
| 5. Electrical | Electro-chemical |
| 6. Must be programmed with new knowledge | Learns on its own |
| 7. Very fast in Computation | Relatively slower in Computation |
| 8. Digital working. Needs step by step method for problem solving. | Extremely good at problem solving. Uses parallel processing or "Search Trees". |
| 9. Memory—Long-term memory. | Forgetful |
| 10. Accurate and Algorithmic | Inaccurate and Heuristic. Needs no external programmer (is meta programmed or pro-grammes itself) |

intelligence (AI) of the silicon chips. The chart below compares Artificial Silicon Intelligence with the Hydrocarbon intelligence of the brain.

The much touted silicon intelligence then turns out to be mere adjunct to Hydrocarbon intelligence. *Its chief functions appears to be to free the hydrocarbon chips of the routine work load of computation and memorization and thereby free them for creative activity and problem solving pursuits.*

The superiority of the Hydrocarbon based neurons over the silicon microchips is staggering. In sheer terms of the density of information storage in a given volume—the neurons of the brain leave the VLSI (very large scale integrated circuits) in the shade. *The human brain is 1000 times as dense as a digital computer.* Volume wise, one litre of it contains 20 billion neurons. The speed of the super computer dazzles us. But it is only the speed of computation. The computer carries out serial processing—that is its CPU (central processing unit) executes calculations one step at a time. Say if you have to add 1000 numbers—the computer will have to perform 1000 individual operations. The speed with which this is done denotes the class of the computer. Transistor switched computers do this in Nano seconds. Transphaser (optical equivalent of transistor) switched computers will do this 1000 times faster-in pico seconds. *To increase speed we have to shorten the path of the current. This calls for miniaturisation and micro miniaturisation.* Hence VLSI and ELSI chips. By the 1990s the highest achievable limit were reached due to limitations of solid-state physics. It is here that an evolutionary cul-de-sac has been reached in basic computer design or architecture. *Basic computer architecture incidentally has not changed since the 1940s when Paul Von Neuman created the basic design based on the Central Processing Unit (CPU).* The main problem today is how to overcome the tyranny of the Single Central

Processor. *This single processor necessitates the step-by-step serialized processing mode.* Problem solving can only be done by this step-by-step basis. We have to flow chart the various steps of the solution. This is called algorithmic programming. *To perform everyday tasks of our daily lives this step-by-step algorithmic approach would take exponential time.* The computer falters and falls way behind the human brain. Unless we can change its basic architecture so that it can operate in a Heuristic mode as the human brain does. For this the two alternative computer architectures being tried are: —

(a)  Parallel Processing Paths: The Cray XMP series (a fourth generation computer) has two processor systems. HEP built by Delne car uses four processors working in parallel. These have achieved speeds of 40 mips (million instructions per second). The US Atomic Energy Commission uses a computer consisting of 8-linked Cray-1 (nick named Octopus). To increase speeds these computers use parallel processing paths where computation is done simultaneously. India has developed the Param Super Computer lately.

(b)  Tree Architecture: In this radical design of computer architecture, processors are arranged like leaves on the branches, which act as a common path to and from the main trunk where data is being organized. Computer programmers have already been using "search trees" that resemble an upside down tree. The root Node is on top and the branches of possibilities bifurcate below as shown in the illustration overleaf.

**THE MYTHICAL KALPA VRIKSHA**
**(The Bao-Bab Tree of Africa?)**
**With Root Above and Branches Below**

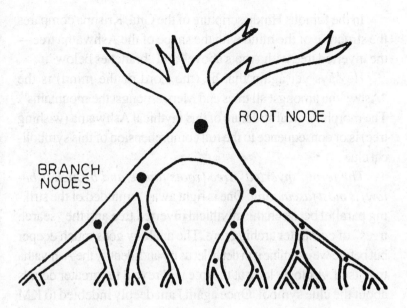

## Kalpavriksha: The Tree Architecture of the Mind

The constructors of species evolution, so it appears, had overcome the Paul Von Neuman bottleneck encountered in computer architecture today, many million of years ago. The neurons of the human brain act as mini processors that are arranged as per the tree architecture. The cerebrospinal axon constitutes the tree trunk pathway of information as it were. Processing is done in tree branch pathways of inter neural connections. The speed with which the human brain solves complex problems of day-to-day existence is phenomenal. It would stump any serialised processor and leave parallel processing in the shade. Curiously enough in the brain neurons themselves, the axons are shaped like the trunks of trees and the Dendrites like branches. The Kundalini as we have seen is one powerful motif that serves as some sort of a Kekule's dream symbol of the true nature of human creativity. Another such seed image from the Indian mythology is the image of the Kalpavriksha—or the mythical wishing tree.

In the famous Hindu scripture of the Gita, Krishna compares the structure of the mind with the shape of the Ashwatha tree—the inverted tree with "roots above" and "branches below".

He says yet again that he (the Lord of the mind) is the "Ashwatha amongst all trees and Meru amongst the mountains". The morphological structure of this mythical Ashwatha (wishing tree) is of consequence to the full comprehension of this symbolical clue.

*The term "inverted" tree (roots above and branches below) is most fascinating.* One is right away reminded of the striking parallel between this mythical inverted tree and the "search trees" of computer architecture. The analogy goes much deeper but before we examine it in detail let us try and identify the Ashwatha tree itself. A closer look at the tree will reveal far greater details about the clue symbol. Once again I am deeply indebted to KM Vaid, the dedicated botanist of the Indian Forest Research Institute of Dehradun. A plant physiologist and a keen photographer, he lived in a house surrounded by tall stately trees. He had once undertaken the quest to identify the mythical Ashwatha or wishing tree (also called the Kalpavriksha) from the morphological descriptions in the classical texts. The Gita describes it as having roots above and branches below. For a time he toyed with the thought that this morphological description best fitted the classical Banyan tree. He was not satisfied. He then went to the Ellora caves in the Southern Maharashtra province of India. These rock caves contain some exquisite sculptures of the Hindu, Jain and Buddhist faiths. One of them depicts the goddess Indrani (consort of Indra—King of the Vedic Gods) seated under the mythical Kalpavriksha. The statue is renowned for its beauty and great accuracy of detail in which each necklace, eyelash and bracelet is carved. The statue of the tree itself is full of details. Vaid assumed that the acute powers of observation displayed by the great sculptures in matter of anatomical, ornamental and structural details should also extend to the morphological details of the tree. The artist, he was sure, had used living models available locally. He therefore made a detailed observation of the morphological details of the tree depicted in the sculpture. He must have spent weeks and days in acute observation. One fine day he walked out into the sunshine and looked up casually at the entrance of the caves. He was struck by a bolt of lightening as it were. There, lo and behold, was the very tree he had been looking for. Botanically it was *the famous Bao-Bab tree, a gigantic tree, which is of African origin. It thrives in the Arusha National Park in Tanzania and elsewhere in Africa. It is massive in size and fantastic in shape. The diameter of its trunk exceeds 80 metres in many cases. When branches shed their leaves, they look as grotesque as bare roots. The tree really and truly gives the impression as if it has been uprooted and placed upside down with roots above and branches beneath the ground.*

*The tree lives for almost 5000 years, perhaps that explains the name "Kalpavriksha"—for "Kalpa" means an age and this tree lives for an entire age of human kind.* A strange variety of breadfruit grows on this tree. It is the favourite food of monkeys. The fruit appears in many fantastic shapes and sizes. *Over a period of time the trunk of the tree becomes hollow and water gets stored within it.* The Africans use it as a well in times of drought and draw water from it. Its bark comes off in layers, which can be used as paper for writing or even as a crude cloth by primitive tribes. Some jungle-folk make their homes inside its hollow tree trunk. For primitive people it must really have been a wish-fulfilling tree. *Ancient Indians had extensive commercial contact with Africa from as far back as the time of the Indus Valley civilization. They must have brought saplings of this wonder tree with them. The Vedic seers gazed at it in awe. In their meditations they had intuitive insights that related its morphological structure in a strange way with the structure of the human mind.* They had predated the successors of Paul Von Neuman by 5000 years.

The analogy of the Kalpavriksha needs far greater reflection. It is a symbol that will reveal much more about the architecture of the mind in the years to come. The more we reflect upon it the more it reveals to us. "The Brains architectural shape is like the Bao-Bab tree"—it sounds like a meaningless Zen Koan. "It has roots above and branches below". *The branches spreading below in the body could be the nerve networks of the central and autonomic nervous system. Roots above? Could this point out to a field view of the mind, a non-physical description that seeks to draw its information inputs from a halo like morphogenetic field or Human Energy Field (HEF) around the brain?* One can only speculate. The more we reflect on this symbol the more will it reveal to us the hidden nature of reality.

*The second clue that the tree architecture provides us is the clue of photosynthesis. The leaves of a tree spread themselves to soak in the sunlight.* The sunlight triggers off the process of photosynthesis from which chlorophyll is manufactured. *Could the neurons of the brain act as leaves that photosynthesise the informational output from the morphogenetic field to produce the Neuro-transmitters and tropic hormones that set the tone for our moods, metabolism and growth?* It is these biochemical secretions that set the endocrine orchestra clanging.

## Boolean Algebra Versus Fractals

Silicon computers are based on the Binary language of Boolean Algebra. They work on two basic digits of "Zero" and "One" (0 and 1). With the help of this binary language code the computers can generate and process awesome amounts of information.

## The Bio-computers

As opposed to this, the bio-computer based on the colloidal chips of the DNA works on a four (as opposed to a two) letter code of A, C, T, G. The complexity of this four-letter code language therefore is far, far greater than the complexity of the two-digit silicon based computers.

## Fractal Forms

When we closely observe nature, we find that its forms are not random and erratic. They are governed by a very superior order of mathematics called Fractals. It is these fractals that enable computers to generate complex images from simple basic forms and repeat the same endlessly over many orders of magnitude and levels. The seemingly random designs of flowers, petals and leaves have an underlying order of Fractal form. From very simple basic structures, very complex micro aggregates can be generated at the macro level.

The only facet that does not lend itself to mathematical analysis is form. Pythagorean Geometry deals with simplified forms that we could master and manipulate mathematically. Nature's infinite repertoire of form however is not constrained by the limitations of Euclidean design. The forms that we encounter in nature are so myriad, diverse and complex that no known discipline of mathematics can account for even a fraction of them. Today however, there is a whole new field of mathematics emerging: Fractals, Phase Portraits and Strange Attractors. These are all analysed within the overall framework of Topology (a branch of mathematics pioneered by Poincare).

The only branch of mathematics that allows us to deal with the repetitive generation of highly complex forms in nature is this new mathematical branch of Fractals. Fractals provide us an insight into how nature probably operates concurrently on many levels of order and form. Computer generated images now seek to replicate the techniques of nature. Natural order and form are fractal in nature.

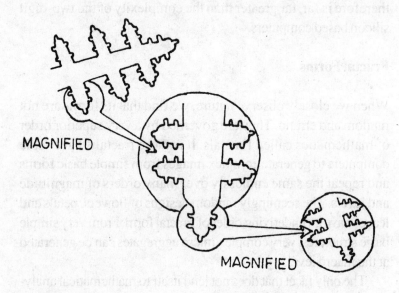

MAGNIFIED

MAGNIFIED

# CHAPTER ELEVEN

## A HOLOGRAMIC UNIVERSE? THE FUSION CORE OF CONCIOUSNESS

John Taylor writing in "The Shape of Minds to come" said, "It is the great size of the frontal lobe of the brain which principally distinguishes the brain of man from that of other animals. *What is the role of the frontal lobes of the brain?* Surprisingly it has no direct control over any physical process in the body. There have been thousands of cases of brain damage where partial or nearly complete loss of the frontal lobes has caused very little change in physical controls or skills. What then is forfeited when the frontal lobes of the brain are destroyed or disconnected? The answer *is a certain cohesion of personality, a certain degree of organization of thoughts and emotions to plan for long range action, especially as required in complex intellectual processes. It seems that CREATIVE work of considerable complexity is a closed book for most patients who have lost their frontal lobes.* Taylor quotes Lord Brian who said: "In considering the function of the frontal lobe then, *we encounter two interweaving strands, time-sense and emotions* and here we reach the roots of personality in which we can say that emotion is binding together past, present and future, or that the *time sense is essential to the integration of emotions with the rest of the mental life.* Perhaps there are two different ways of saying the same thing".

Over the years a rather simplistic structure of the brain had become popular in the West. In keeping with the Newtonian Cartesian Paradigm current in our age, it glorified rational thought as more evolved and classed emotions as the more archaic remnants of our evolutionary past. This led the American scientist *Paul MacLean to argue that the brain has three layers that betray its evolutionary past as layered rocks reveal the story of the earths crust.* He called these layers: —

(a) **Reptilian:** The reptilian brain is the hindbrain and midbrain and is slave to precedent.

(b) **Paleomamalian or Old Mammalian Brain**. This comprises the structures on top of the brain stem (Hypothalamus, Limbic system and Amygdala). This is the seat of emotions.

(c) **Neo Mammalian or New Mammalian Brain:** This comprises of the cortex and is supposed to be the seat of the higher evolutionary functions of Reason.

This rational "bias" has made scientist oversimplify what is a higher complex structure. As is evident, the cortex is not only the seat of reason, memory, language abilities and abstraction but also helps mediate the higher emotions. The frontal lobes in particular have a crucial bearing upon the nature of man's personality, that mixture of emotional character and thought. It is here that time sense and emotions seem to fuse in a strange amalgam. Evidently personality involves interaction between large areas of the cortex and the limbic system that older inner emotional brain. Herb (1966 as quoted by R Mel Zack and Casey in the Loyola symposium on feelings and emotions) has *emphasized the role of memory and experience in emotions in which the cerebral cortex is involved. The remembered outcome of previous actions and past experience with similar configurations of events is critical in determining our reactions in emotional situations".*

## The Hologramic Theory of Memory and Abstract Thought

The nature of the cortex is quite mystifying. Each point of it has been thoroughly mapped and probed with electrodes. There is a great amount of redundancy built into its structure. Once one portion is damaged, neighbouring areas take on its function in a matter of time. This is best illustrated by the phenomena of memory storage. Experimental evidence shows that memory is not confined to any particular areas of the brain cortex but are distributed throughout. Wilber Penfield's Electrical Stimulation of the Brain experiments has elicited vivid recall of past experiences when various points of the cortex were stimulated with electrodes. These vivid recalls relived the past experiences as it were with a complete replay of the visual, audio, olfactory and tactile impressions recorded then. Within the few hundred cubic centimetres volume of the brain cortex are stored millions upon millions of bits of memory and information. *No known physical process can account for this density of information storage is in so small a volume. This had led Carl Pibram to propose a revolutionary new theory that memory and abstract thoughts are like holograms. Incoming visual and auditory pathways converge and interfere in the cortex permanently encoding experience as a chemical memory trace on nerve pathways.* The interference pattern of bioelectrical currents set up in the brain by the incoming visual auditory and tactile stimuli is recorded as a hologram in the brain cortex. These memories can be recalled for the purpose of abstract thought and like a hologram, which holds the entire image on every chip of its plate, *damage to the brain may not result in the loss of remembered experience.* Pibram has suggested that memory is diffused along the entire cortex but not like a photo plate. *The electrical waves that proceed along the synapses record these in a hologram fashion.* He has suggested Fourier's wave analysis as a possible modus operandi for this recording process. Fourier's wave analysis breaks down complex waves into simpler sine waves for storage in the hologramic memory circuits.

## The Intriguing Nature of the Hologram and the Question of Immortality

The Greek word "Holos" (whole) and gramma (a letter) were combined to give the modern world a new word "Hologram" or the "whole message". The word was coined by the Hungarian born British Nobel Laureate Dr Dennis Gabor, who invented the technique of holography in 1948. Recognition for it came in the form of the Nobel Prize almost three decades later, when the invention of lasers enabled Gabor's theories to be translated into practice. The technical name for Holography is Wave Front Reconstruction. *Holography works with any waves, electron, sound or light.* It is a fascinating discovery. What exactly is a hologram? In many ways it is the reverse of a photograph. A beam of monochromatic (laser) light is split into two by a mirror arrangement. One of these split beams (called the object beam) is used to light up the object to be recorded. The other beam (called reference beam) is kept undisturbed. The object beam falls on the object and an interference wave pattern is produced as the light waves strike it and are scattered by it. This interference pattern is then mixed with the original reference beam. Like waves converging on a beach, it forms a diffraction grating pattern of light and dark interference bands as the two waves interact with each other. This resultant interference pattern is directly recorded on a photographic plate. When developed, the photograph looks like a meaningless fingerprint of light and dark bands that bears no resemblance to the original object. However if the same beam of monochromatic light is passed through this plate, it gives rise to an astonishing three-dimensional image of the object, an image in its original depth and detail, exactly as if a real wave front from the object had reached our eyes (a wave front contains information about direction and intensity of the light pattern). Holograms and the images they produce have some dramatic properties besides three-dimensional realism. *The most fascinating of them is the indestructibility of the hologram. If we cut the Hologram in half, it will still produce the whole image. In fact any fragment of the Hologram can produce the entire image*—even if the fragment is extremely small. This is because light waves from every spot on the object interact with the reference beam and are recorded everywhere on the film. *Theoretically each molecule of it contains the whole information. It is the part that contains the whole. It is a record that is indestructible.*

It is this property that led Carl Pibram to propose that *abstract thought and memory are hologramic in nature.* No other physical process can explain this density of information storage in the few hundred cubic centimetres of the cortex. It is this that explains the indestructibility of our memories for they are spread everywhere throughout the cortex. Apparently they are immortal in a way, as all Holograms are immortal.

## Cross Wiring of the Brain

There is more to this Hologramic theory than just a mere analogy. *A detailed study of the "wiring pattern" of the nerve networks in our brains indicates a cross wiring pattern that is tailor-made to produce interference between the object beam and the original reference beam (or bio-electrical impulse).* This cross wiring pattern goes right through. As we know there are two lobes of the brain—the Left Hemisphere and the Right Hemisphere. The Left Hemisphere controls the right portion of the body and vice-versa. The various nerves affect a grand crossing over in the Brain stem (so called Reptilian brain). *Millions of nerve fibres (cortico–spinal tracts) switch sides in the grand crossing over called cortico spinal Decussation.* Bundles of sensory nerves from the left side of the body have shifted to the right side of the brain while bundles of motor nerves from the right side of the brain have shifted to the left side of the brain and vice-versa.

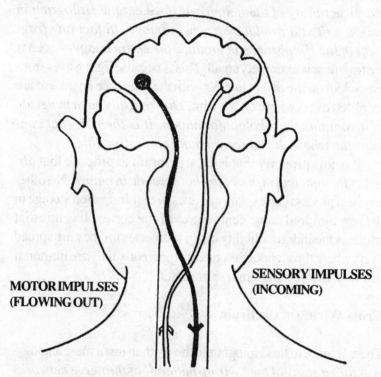

**MOTOR IMPULSES (FLOWING OUT)**

**SENSORY IMPULSES (INCOMING)**

**Optic Chiasma:** The most *dramatic application of this cross wiring pattern is found in the physiology of vision.* Light falls on the eyes—it enters via the pupil and is bent (inverted) by the lens and made to fall on the retina. Here it causes minute bioelectrical currents to originate in the photoreceptor cells. This current travels down the thick optic nerves that link the eyes with the back of the cerebral hemisphere. Near the back of the eyes both optic nerves meet in *the so-called optic–chiasma ("crossing").* Here nerve fibres from the part of each retina nearest the nose cross over. Thus the resulting left optic tract carries data about objects from the RIGHT hand side of the field of vision and the right optic tract takes signals from the object seen on the left. These signals pass through the Thalamus and optic radiation area on to the visual screen formed in the near portion of the brain hemisphere where they are perceived. A portion of each optic tract carries original "reference" information from its originating side. The diagrams illustrate this best.

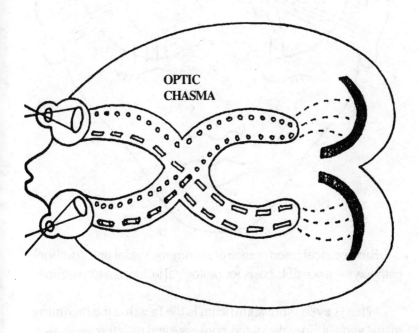

OPTIC
CHASMA

The input from the inside portion of the eyes crosses over while that from the outer fringes does not and forms the original reference beam as it were. Interference is achieved in the optic chiasma region.

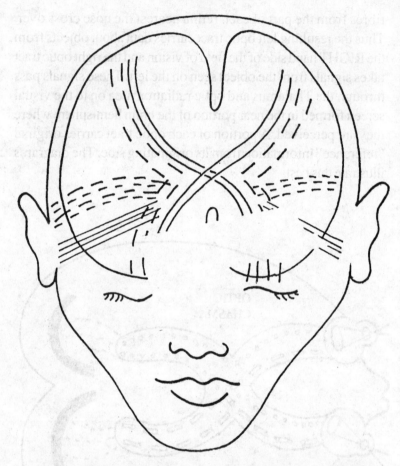

Bioelectrical interference of incoming Visual and Auditory pathways—a possible basis for biological hologram formation?

What is even more significant is the fact that the incoming visual and auditory pathways converge and interfere as shown, thus setting up interference pattern in bioelectrical waves generated in the brain. These appear to be recorded in the cortex chemically (Caplan–Fodrin Cascade) as memory traces. Perhaps the three dimensional reality that we perceive about us is hologramically generated in our brains.

## Imagination

Creative imagination is the most wonderful gift of evolution in mankind. It is this, which gives man his capability of abstraction. *The word imagination comes from the word image. It is the faculty that enables man to form internalised images.* Many years ago *McDougall had proposed the imagic theory of instincts. Central to each instinct he felt, is an image of its object. Thus central to the sexual instinct is an image of the female of the species.* Linking this with the hologramic theory of thought and images, it is possible that the images of our imagination faculties are equally hologramic. So are our thoughts and memories and instinctual images. *In the curious way of holograms, these are indestructible. The speculation about an indestructible hologramic core of our personalities then becomes an intriguing possibility. Is it possible that our personalities are structured around a hologramic reservoir of inherited images that are either genetically transmitted or otherwise perpetuating themselves in ways difficult to understand?* Could we speculate that these hologramic image reservoirs are held in the morphogenetic or form generating field as a record of interference pattern in the bio-plasma? The nature of the field is hologramic. *It is the source of all instinctual images. It tells the bees how to build their hives, the birds how to build their nests.* It guides the growth of body cells to achieve predetermined shapes.

## The Fusion Core of Consciousness

*Somewhere in the cores of our brains lie our deep-seated emotions and animal instincts—in the Hypothalamus, Limbic system and Amygdala—in the reptilian core of our consciousness. Somewhere in the fore brain lobes, the emotions fuse with our time-sense and in a strange way bind together our past, present and future.* As we peer deeper into the mind we seem to encounter a fusion core deep within where these emotions seem to fuse and melt into one another. Love mixes with hate, pain with pleasure in strange fusion and amalgams that seem to take place in what Freud has called the unconscious or the ID. If our thoughts and memories are hologramically generated, then it is plausible that these interference patterns mix and interact with the pre-existing recorded traces. The Fusion core is hologramic in nature. The observed psychological fact of the fusion or amalgams of emotions seem to indicate a fusion core in the reactors of our consciousness. There is also an energic basis apart from the hologramic network of bioelectrical ripples in the brain, which constantly interfere to create fantastic wave patterns and diffraction bands in the brain. *This fusion core is the source of all synthesis; this is the "Gayatri" or the inner sun of our beings.* Just as Hydrogen atoms fuse into Helium and cause the sun to blaze and burn in primordial splendour—so also ideas, concepts, thoughts, images, moods, and emotions fuse and blend in the core of our minds to produce a furnace for creative synthesis of a marvellous kind.

### Emotions: The Power Behind Our Drives

The fusion of emotions provides the real source of power to the reactors of our consciousness. For *emotions are the real energic components of our psyche. They are the energic fusing elements, "the glue that binds together the universe", the real power behind all our drives.* Writing in the Loyalla la Symposium on emotions (1970) (Feelings and Emotions), Silvan S Tompkins of New Jersey described Affect or emotion as the primary motivational system. He wrote, *"It has been deemed that the biological drives are the primary sources of motivations of all animals including man. This is a radical error. The intensity, the urgency, the imperiousness, the "umph" of drives is an illusion. The illusion is created by the misidentification of the drive "signal" with its "amplifier". Its amplifier is the affective (emotional) response which is ordinarily recruited to "boost the gain" of the drive signal".*

*"Thus it is emotions rather than instinctual drives which are the primary human motives. This primacy is demonstrated by the fact that the drive requires amplification from the affects (emotion) wherein the emotions are sufficient motivation in the absence of drives. One must be excited to be sexually aroused but one need not be sexually aroused to be excited.* We misidentify the tumescence of the sexual drive with the affect (emotion) of excitement. *Excitement is recruited as the amplifier of the sexual drive signal.* Those who are generally bored with each other may also be unable to become sexually excited even when *they are capable* of stimulating tumescence and orgasm" (Loyola Symposium on Feelings and Emotions). In terms of radio technology we have the information signal, which is grafted on to the "carrier" signal for transmission. *Emotions are the carrier signals that are recruited to amplify the basic drives. These drives may be the four basic needs to breathe, to eat, to drink and sex.* These also extend to more intellectual problem solving pursuits. As the "Eureka whoop" of Archimedes reveals, *the basic amplifier or carrier signals of emotions (our inner power house) must be recruited as the energic basis of all our endeavours in life.*

From the understanding of the link between the thought matrices of a simple joke to the solution of a scientific puzzle or problem or a complex mathematical equation: from the gentle empathising response in the viewing of a tragedy or the emotional violence that fuels a revolution, all our basic drives and human pursuits have to be fed from the fuels of our emotional powerhouse. "Enthusiasm" so felt the Greeks, "was the God within".

*Emotions are the energic fuels of our psyche; they are the energic aspects of our consciousness. In biochemical terms they are translated as our Neuro-peptides and enkephalins, as the Neuro-transmitters and tropic hormones that fuel our drives. The biochemical determinants of emotions are well known. Thus Testosterone, a male hormone accentuates Para sympathetic lust. Adrenaline is intimately connected with sympathetic Rage and Fear.* Adrenalin exists in two forms Adrenalin A and B. Adrenalin A is secreted from the medulla of the adrenal gland to the blood stream. Doses of it when injected into human beings *have caused the reaction of anxiety. This Adrenalin A abounds in timid animals like rabbits, guinea pigs and herbivores in general. Adrenalin B is secreted at the Adrenal nerve endings of the sympathetic nerves. It predominates in carnivores and leads to the fight or aggression response.* The quality of the inner biochemical landscape shapes the external experience, outlook and total life style of the organism. It moulds the personality of the human beings.

**Emotional Polarity**

Kruger, the Gestalt psychologist, had envisaged a basic polarity of emotions. This comprised the dimensions of

    (a)  Intensity
    (b)  Depth

**Intensity** This may be expressed in terms of *vehemence rather than personal relevance.* They occur as emotional explosions that are intense, short lived but surface phenomena. Rage for instance *is such a surface outburst.* Anguish over a loved one's death is another such example.

    Depth *Death on the other hand creates a profound emotional experience that touches a man's psychological existence, his metaphysical core.* These occur on an entirely different and deeper level than his normal life. Intense experiences are short-lived. Profound experiences are long lasting, often affecting a whole lifetime. The classic example of such depth emotional experience is the Buddha witnessing old age, disease and death. They affected the core of his being and altered him profoundly. *In general, explosiveness of emotions seems opposed to depth of emotions. Sensitivity is a depth phenomenon, sentimentality an intensity phenomenon. Friendship, love, loyalty to one's country can be depth phenomena.* They pervade a lifetime. Thus depression as direction less mood has depth, sorrow or sadness over a loved one's death has intensity. *Hate is a depth phenomenon—it may smoulder for a whole lifetime.* Intensity may be mobilized against depth. An emotional flare up may be used consciously or unconsciously to silence deeper levels of feeling (man defends himself against sorrow by rage).

The subjective experience of emotions then can be analysed under the dimensions of depth and intensity. Intensity is in terms of the quantum of bio-chemicals released, the massive dosage of adrenalin which triggers an out burst of rage. These are *based upon the body and the quantum of its hormonal fuels available and mobilized for a particular situation.* The neurons fire off; the endocrine glands secrete and must recuperate. Intensity can never be long lasting. It needs to recover, it needs to build up its biochemical levels—it needs recuperation for a remobilisation of essences. In depth we are sinking or diving from the surface or body consciousness level into the Fusion core of our psychological existence. Diving into a magma where emotions fuse with time sense and bind with memories to form that magic amalgam of human personality, the very core of our aliveness—the volcanic substratum of energy that seems to lie at the basis of our body-mind complex. Its keynote is Fusion and synthesis—it is Holistic. Quite possibly it is a field phenomena of the order of the proposed Informational Energy Field or Sheldrake's Morphogenetic field. The hologramic interference patterns and wave fronts reside in the field. They represent the wave aspect of reality not its particle mode.

## The Emotional Memory Matrix

"Krueger (1928) and Klager (1950), from the point of view of the Gestalt school, emphasized that *feelings and emotions are integral parts of perception. Krueger insisted that every kind of activity, even the most abstract intellectual judgment grows out of a background of feeling. Feelings provide the MATRIX connecting all other experiences.*

*The linkage between stimulus and response depends upon memory.* Every new situation recalls familiar situations experienced in the past and their effect on us. When we recall them we experience them in visual, auditory, tactual, motor and even olfactory modalities. We recall a picture we have seen, a tune we have heard, and a scent we have cherished. We also relive the pain, the joys, and the sorrows we felt in the past.

*The emotional (Affective) memory is intensely personal because it is the living record of the emotional life history of each person.* Being always at our disposal, playing an important role in the appraisal and interpretation of everything around us, it can be called the matrix of all experience and action (Magda B Arnold in the Loyola Symposium). This emotional memory matrix is a hologramic energic reservoir that may not just be confined to frontal lobes of the brain cortex. It may well have a non-physical dimension. In the Jungian scheme of things an *emotion has been defined as a total event of the personality, activating all levels and therefore a symbolic kind of transformed consciousness with "body" in it.* It is a heightened condition. An emotional complex may be defined as a group of psychic contents inter twined in a specific pattern and cohesively united by a similar affective tone. They are affect (emotion laden). *Like affects they are "ego-alien".* We experience them as intruders. We, not only have them but they have us. The archetypal core of the complex is an instinctual pattern of behaviour and an image idea. (James Hillman, Loyola Symposium). The hologramic image idea expresses this beautifully.

## Multi Dimensional Model of Emotions

Robert Plutchik of the Albert Einstein College of medicine had proposed a multi-dimensional model of emotions as shown below. This catered for the depth and intensity of emotions and explained how they were likely to mix.

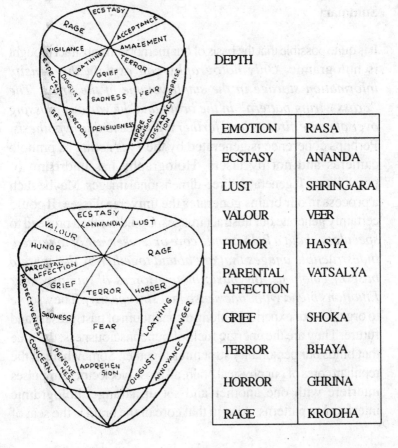

DEPTH

| EMOTION | RASA |
|---|---|
| ECSTASY | ANANDA |
| LUST | SHRINGARA |
| VALOUR | VEER |
| HUMOR | HASYA |
| PARENTAL AFFECTION | VATSALYA |
| GRIEF | SHOKA |
| TERROR | BHAYA |
| HORROR | GHRINA |
| RAGE | KRODHA |

This diagrammatic model arrangement shows the polarity of emotions in a different way. Thus ecstasy is the opposite of grief, rage of terror, loathing of acceptance. Adjacent emotions mix easily, opposites do not. Thus ecstasy mixes easily with rage or acceptance, terror with amazement or grief but grief does not bind with ecstasy. Along the vertical dimension this model indicates the intensity of that emotion. This model deals with life's basic emotions. The classical model of *Indian art and aesthetics deals with the nine "rasas" or elixirs of life. These represented the entire range or spectrum of emotional experience.* These could also be expressed in terms of the same model.

## Summary

It is quite possible that the basis of our memory and abstract thought is hologramic. *Only holography can explain the density information storage in the small volume of the brain. The "cross wiring pattern" in the brain and the various crossing over of nerve circuits lend further credence to this hypothesis.* Perhaps coherence is generated by the eyes acting as pinhole cameras and not by lasers. Holography has undreamt of possibilities. It generates three-dimensional images. Maybe such a process in our brains generates the universe we see. It could certainly generate our abstract images. Could we then proceed to *speculate about a hologramic core or a reservoir of inherited, indestructible images that are bound together by the energic base of emotions, the basic motive forces of our psyches? Emotions blend with time sense in a strange way.* They serve to organize our experience along a continuum of past, present and future. They are the energic fuels of our consciousness, the glue that binds our personality structures together. Somewhere in the reptilian cores of our physical brain, all those bioelectrical impulses interfere with one another and set up strange, hologramic interference patterns. Also in that core of the brain is the seat of our emotions, that driving powerhouses of our psyches—the basic motive forces of consciousness. The core of energy where all synthesis takes place—just as fusion takes place in the core of the sun.

Maybe, once we learn more about this fusion core of our consciousness and its hologramic nature—we can speculate about an indestructible basis of our personalities; a *hologramic core of instinctual images, and memories all bound together by the energy fuels or complexes of emotions. Possibly that was what the ancient seers meant by the "Atman". When they spoke in riddles and paradoxes about the relation of the Brahman and Atman as the one that has become the many* and yet remains the one that contains all. *The part contains the whole.* It is tempting to speculate that *the ancient seers were confusedly trying to point out to the hologramic nature of reality, where in a para-doxical way, the part does contain the whole and all informa-tion is indestructible.* The relation between the Atman and Brah-man therefore is entirely hologramic.

The spokes of a wheel converge and meet at its Nave. The rays of the Sun diverge from a point of origin in all directions. Their convergence lies at its core. A Vedic verse says:

"Vena the wise has entered the Cave
where all things assume a single form".

This cave is the ventricle of our brain. As per the Vedas—the 'cortical rider", the psychic being, the hologramic Atman resides here. He is thumb-shaped flame, without beginning and end. He is the eternal hologram. Once we enter this cave, we find a region of maximum convergence, fusion and synthesis. All audio, visual, tactile bioelectrical impulses fuse here in a strange alchemy of consciousness. Vena has entered the cave where all things assume a single form. This is the region of maximal synthesis and inner coherence. Is this the source of the biological coherence of our beings? Is this the hologram of cosmic consciousness that forms the core of our individual existence? Is this indestructible hologram the core of our immortal personalities? Is this the cortical rider that goes from life to life?

One is reminded of the immortal dialogue between the sages Angira and Shaunak that occurs in the Atharva Veda.

The sage Shaunak said to the great Rishi Angira.

"Lord which is that science having known
which all else is known?"
"That" replied the sage Angira", is the Science of Brahman. Having known that all else is known".

It is in the human core of consciousness therefore that we encounter the knowledge and Science of Brahman and rediscover the lost secret of our immortality.

# CHAPTER TWELVE

## THE MORPHOGENETIC FIELDS: AN EMERGING SYSTEMS VIEW OF LIFE

The emerging concept of the morphogenetic fields (or the informational energy fields) lies at the core of the major paradigm shift that is likely to occur in the life sciences. Passing references to this emergent concept of the "systems view of life" have been made at many places in this book. It is time to take a more detailed look at this subject.

We can view the ancient Kundalini concept as an attempt (through a structured programme of psycho-somatic exercises) to acquire conscious control of our endocrine system and the deeper cores of our brains. With this acquired control, a desired harvest of Neuro-transmitters and hormones can be secreted to significantly alter the inner biochemical landscape. This biochemical oriented view, though scientifically accurate does not transcend the mechanistic paradigm of yester-years. It only enlightens us about the observed effects and not the underlying causes. For these we have to go beyond the molecular level. To account for the enormous amounts of information transfer, we have no option but to speculate about an Informational—Energy field from which these vast amounts of information and order proceed. Biological form also proceeds from such "form-generating fields". Emotions are one energic aspect of our psyche for which the molecular level effects by themselves do not provide adequate explanation.

For emotions have a baffling energic aspect and a fusion aspect that interweaves them closely with our time perception. These energic charges at the cores of our consciousness have an: "ego-alien" aspect. They appear as intruders in our psychological land-scape. They have power and wondrous strength. They seem to arise from a fusion core at the basis of our beings—An inner "sun of synthesis". *The imagic synthesis takes place in a hologramic fashion in the depths of our brains.* In coming visual, auditory, olfactory, motor and sensory impulses blend and *fuse with one another, as in the heart of a blazing fusion reactor.* These scat-tered images, insights and glimpses that we have outlined in earlier chapters, now need to be bound together firmly by an all-encom-passing theory: a theory that will synthesise these diverse strands of impressions. We need to take an intellectual leap into the future and *propose a field model of human consciousness. We need to transcend the mechanistic model based solely upon the biochemistry of our brains.* For that does not give us the holistic over view of the "unified theory" of consciousness that we need to develop to weave together all the strands of the diverse insights that we have been struggling to obtain. We will, in this chapter therefore, examine more closely the emerging systems view of life. Based upon this radically different view of life, we will at-tempt another reinterpretation of the Kundalini motif. The brain centred theories of the Neuro-biology of all mystical experience, the effervescence of the Neuro-transmitters that leads to ecstasy, does provide insights about the biological basis of this phenom-enon. It tells us what happens at the physical level of reality. But it does not convey the whole truth. What happens at the physical level perhaps is the end product of a cascade of events that ema-nate from the energic levels of the Human Energy Field. It is nec-essary to speculate about such a field to complete our study of these phenomena and build a plausible theory that links effects to their true causes.

## The Morphogenetic Fields

The revolutionary concept of the morphogenetic fields was propounded by the British Plant physiologist Rupert Sheldrake in his Book published in 1981 *"A New Science of Life"*. The book presented such a revolutionary new Paradigm of the life sciences that some in the conventional scientific community turned hysterical. A prestigious scientific journal certified it as a "book fit for burning". The hysterical reaction was rather reminiscent of the famous episode of book burning in Chinese history. A number of other prestigious scientific journals however have lent respectful credence to Dr. Sheldrake views. For in the main Dr Sheldrake has propounded a theory verifiable by the strict scientific methods of experimentation. He has proposed a number of experiments that have been taken up quite enthusiastically in Europe and America. Sheldrake's revolutionary theory is an umbrella concept to explain hitherto unresolved mysteries in many diverse fields. Let us see a few of them: —

**Embryology:** We have already seen how life begins as a single fertilised cell. These cells multiply by a process of fission, which produces a number of identical cells. Each of these identical cells has the same genetic code. However, later they differentiate themselves to form eyes, legs, nose, ears, brain, lungs, heart and kidneys etc. How do these cells "know" what to do? How is the full genetic programme in the DNA of these cells blocked to permit organ specialisation? *Sheldrake felt there had to be some other factor that guided the cells of an embryo towards their respective final form. There was, as it were, an already existing blue print for the form of say a cat and the cells of a feline embryo would grow according to that blue print. Sheldrake reduced the entire issue to a question of form—the structure and shape that a particular object takes up. Sheldrake* *theorised that a living object had a field associated with it.* A field whose nature was determined by the form of that object—just as the nature of a magnetic field depends upon the magnet causing it. This morphogenetic field—like a magnetic field, cannot be seen, heard, touched or smelt. However, Sheldrake pointed out a key difference between the magnetic field and the morphogenetic field. A magnetic field depends upon the existence of the magnet. A morphogenetic field persisted whether the original object remained in existence or not. These morphogenetic fields constitute the basic blue prints of life.

**Information Energy Fields**

Dr Victor Benedict Arul, an Indian microbiologist working in the USA has independently come to the same formulation by applying the mathematical tenets of the information theory to living systems. In his epoch making paper entitled "A new paradigm for the unification of science", Dr Arul has proposed the existence of an informational complex existing in "Space-Bio energy" that serves as the Blueprint of life. He calls it "Information Energy Field". It is this field that provides the informational stimuli for organising the cells of the living organism. These informational fields are the bio-energic matrices or the Force Field blueprints that serve as the basis of life. They provide the informational inputs that determine the shape and structure of the living organisms. Dr Arul's study was primarily aimed at establishing the causes and origin of the dreaded disease of cancer. *Dr Arul theorised that cancer occurs when informational inputs from the field are blocked in a particular organ of the body.* In the absence of these organising inputs the cells begin to grow erratically and haphazardly—thus leading to cancer. The field thus provides the blueprint for the cellular structure of the body.

## Migration of Birds

(a)  There are a number of other fields, which Rupert Sheldrake's umbrella concept of the morphogenetic field serves to explain. How, for instance, do birds that have never been on a transcontinental voyage—know their migratory route? How do they navigate so unerringly over thousands upon thousands of miles? This has so far been an unexplained mystery. Science has failed to unravel the navigation mechanism in the bird's brain. The morphogenetic field theory offers plausible explanations.

(b)  **Formative Causation and Morphic Resonance.** *How do crystals unerringly assume the same form and shape?* Take the example of the moment when a chemical crystal is about to take a particular form. *According to the theory of formative causation put forth by Sheldrake, the morphogenetic field from the crystals of that chemical formed in the past steps across space and time and guides the molecule towards the same form.* Sheldrake calls it the process of *morphic resonance.* This is a spectacular intellectual feat that may one-day rank on par with Einstein's theories of relatively in its epoch making stature. Subsequently in this book we will return to this phenomena of morphic resonance in more detail. As spelt out earlier, Sheldrake's conception of Morphic Resonance is driven by the past. Past mutations are transmitted by the digital language of genes. The shapes and pattern from the past, step across quantum mechanically to structure the present. Ilya Prigogrine and other scientists now tell us that the unidirectional arrow of time can be reversed. Some five millenniums ago, the Vedic seers had theorised about the Kala Agni in our beings; about the Fire or Energy of time, which can be kinetised and reversed. Once the arrow of time is reversed our biologic beings are no longer driven by the past mutations. They are now pulled by the future shapes and possibilities. The future, not the past of the organism, steps across quantum mechanically to guide the present. The organism becomes a prophetic life form.

Learning Theory: This is the scientifically verifiable aspect of Sheldrake's theory and places it on a firm scientific footing. Rupert Sheldrake carried out experiments on rats, who were taught to run mazes. He proved it statistically that once one set of rats had learnt to run the maze successfully, all other rats—anywhere in the world, would take that much lesser time to learn to run that maze. Accelerative and procedural memories, so it appears, propagate in the morphogenetic field universally. Once a particular skill has been learnt by humans (or animals) anywhere on the planet, all other humans (or animals) will learn it with demonstrably and measurably greater ease. Once the human being learns how to drive a car, all other homo sapiens will learn to drive with demonstrably greater ease. Interesting experiments have been conducted on learning rhymes in foreign languages. Once somebody somewhere has learned something, say a poem,, others will find it that much easier to learn it than the first person. And the more often it is learnt, the easier it will become for others to memorise it later. One is strongly reminded of Gary Zukov's assertion in the bestseller "The Dancing Wu Li Masters". *"Information seems to get around real fast in the field"*. The revolutionary aspect is that these field phenomena do not seem to be subject to the inverse square law. All these people who learnt that poem (including the first one) could be separated by thousands of kilometres or decades and centuries and yet the end result would be the same.

## The Immune System: Overriding Proof of the Field Theory

Perhaps the most convincing argument for the morphogenetic or Informational Energy Field point of view would be the Human

Immune System. It is a miracle of human evolution. It is nature's most vibrant example of creative problem solving. The immune system is not controlled by any central organ such as the brain. Rather it has developed to function as some sort of a biologic democracy wherein the individual members achieve their ends through an information network of awesome scope. The Immune Response may be considered to have four steps: —

(a) Recognition of the enemy
(b) Amplifications of Defence
(c) Attack
(d) Slow down (turning off) and memorisation (Immunologi cal memory).

The body's immune defence is based on white blood cells. These account for one percent of the body's 100 billion cells and arise in the bone marrow. These are of the following classes as shown in diagram.

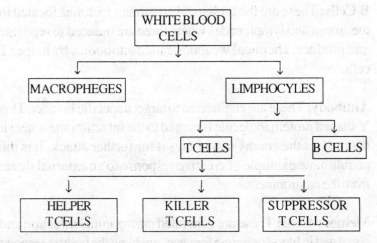

The functioning of these individual cells will best explain the working of the human immune system. As said there are two types of white blood cells—Macrophages and Lymphocyles: —

**Macrophages:** These eat up foreign cells and summon the helper
T Cells.

**Lymphocyles:** These are of two main classes, T cells and B cells.
T cells are of three types:

(a)  Helper T Cells: Are the commanders of the Immune system. They identify the "enemy" (the self and non-self) and
rush to the spleen or nymph nodes to stimulate production
of other cells to fight infection.

(b)  Killer T Cells: Activated by helper T cells, these specialise
in killing foreign cells as well as cancer cells.

(c)  Suppressor T Cells: This third type of T cells is able to slow
down or stop the activities of B or other T cells and play a
vital role in calling off the attack after an infection has been
conquered.

**B Cells:** These are the biological armament factories located in
the spleen and lymph nodes where these are induced to replicate
and produce, chemical weapons called antibodies by helper T
cells.

**Antibody:** These are engineered to target a specific invader. This
Y shaped protein molecule is rushed to the infection site where it
neutralises the enemy cell or tags it for further attack. It is the
penultimate example of creative response to an external threat
from the environment.

**Memory Cells:** These are generated during initial infection and
circulated in blood or lymph for years, enabling the body to respond
more quickly to subsequent infection. These are largely peptides
and form the basis of the Immunological memory. They provide

the molecular basis for an information system of awesome complexity.

**Lymphokines:** The immune system is a vast and highly complex information system where the signalling is done by Protein messengers called Lymphokines which stimulate the production of T cells and also signal the brain to raise body temperature (* 1L-1 and 1L-2 Gamma interferon). All this forms a vast and well-coordinated orchestra of intricate stimulus and response chains. The management of information at all levels of the immune response and the feed back loops which help to call off the immune response once the infection has been neutralised, lead one to wonder. Is all this possible without theorising about a general Informational energy field that handles and processes this vast amount of information? It would be essential to apply the tenets of the information theory to the workings of living organisms.

**Thoughts and the Immune System:** Recent researchers have shown that depressive moods depress or impair the response of the immune system and make the body vulnerable to infection. Psychological stress or anxiety seems to impair the effectiveness of immune system. Psycho immunology is fast becoming an interesting new field of research. These serve to highlight the clear linkages between the "Mind" and the Immune system.

**Neuro-Peptides and Immune System:** Stress stimulates secretion of Neuro-peptides, which influence moods and emotions. Endorphins kill pain and cause euphoria. Research has indicated that endorphins fit snugly into receptors of lymphokines, thereby suggesting a direct route through which "mind" could influence immunity. Researches at the National institute of Health in Bethesda Maryland have *indicated that macrophages themselves actually release Neuro peptides. These scavenging white blood cells may also serve as free-floating nerve cells able to communicate* *with the brain. Neuro-peptides play a major role in the learning process.* The vast complexity and volume of the information traffic involved in the immune system and its linkage with the secretions of neuro-peptides serves as the most convincing argument for the existence of a highly complex information field existing in space-bio-energy and managing the complex flow of information through signals that secrete protein messengers, lymphokines Neuro-transmitters and neuro-peptides. Information is transferred in terms of these biochemical signals that constitute a language of great complexity. In brief then, the Immune system helps us to recognise the self from the non-self. The Immune system detects the intruder based on establishing this identity of the self from the non-self. It identifies the non-self intruder and tags it for attack. It then launches the attack—determines the chemical composition of the intruder—manufactures the right anti-toxin for its neutralisation or destruction. It then calls off the attack once the intruder has been killed. The response is then stored in the immunological memory. What we see at work therefore is a highly coherent information system of awesome complexity. It is possibly the best argument for the existence of bio-energy fields or Morphogenetic fields that exist in space bio-energy and are the basis of our biologic forms.

Biologic forms, as stated earlier, are like whirlpools. Just as the water in a whirlpool is in constant motion and change but the form of the whirlpool remains constant, so also, living systems maintain a constant form even as the matter in them, the molecules and atoms are changing over continually. It is the hypothesis of these forms—generating fields that explain the constancy of biological forms.

## The Working Model

The basic blue prints of all life forms are provided by the Morphogenetic Fields. They exist as informational complexes in "space-bio energy" and give rise to the living organisms by providing the informational and organising stimuli to the molecular and cellular levels of life. They provide the coded instructions that act upon the DNA and RNA chains of our cells. They provide the trigger signals that unleash pre-wired genetic programmes as also the filter signals that permit organ specialisation in particular cells. These Fields are the basis of the body's form and structures. It is their informational inputs that ensure its coherent functioning and maintain its order.

## Body Field Symmetry

The body and the field occupy the same complex in space-time. They are co-located. The field permeates the body. These informational energy fields are symmetrical in shape to the human (animal or plant) bodies that they give rise to. There is a very close level of correspondence from organ to organ. Informational inputs from the field cause the body cells to grow in an organised manner. The body therefore is more or less an exact molecular replica of the field. Absence or blockage of field informational inputs can lead to cancer in that effected organ site, which is deprived of its informational in put from the field. In the absence of this information it looses its biological order. The cancerous growth thereafter is erratic, entropic and disorderly. It becomes life threatening for the organism. The Morphogenetic Fields therefore sustain the form, order and coherence of a biological system. It is, as Ilya Prigogrine tells us, a system far from equilibrium. A living system is so unlike a machine. In a machine (say a bicycle or car) the parts are designed, manufactured and put together to form a structure with fixed components. In a living system the contrast is marked. The components change ceaselessly but the essential form nevertheless remains constant. To highlight the seemingly paradoxical existence of change and stability, Ilya

Prigogrine coined the term "Dissipative structures". A French physicist, Henry Benard had discovered that the heating of a thin layer of liquid may result in the spontaneous formation of strangely ordered patterns and structures. A very striking ordered pattern of hexagonal (Honeycomb) like cells appear in which hot liquid rises through the centre of the cells while the cooler liquid descends along the cell walls. This Benard instability is a spectacular example of spontaneous self-organising action. Living systems are now being studied in terms of synthesis of the aspects of pattern with structure or form.

### Field Flux Density

Like all force fields the morphogenetic field should comprise of innumerable lines of force. The Flux density of this morphogenetic field should be highest along the central carbo-spinal axis of the field. Theoretically the flux density should reduce gradually towards the periphery of the field. *The lines of force could also serve as the blue print for the growth of the skeletal, muscular and nervous systems and systems for the circulation of blood and lymph in the body.* These lines of force could have close correspondence with the yogic conception of Nadis or the Acupuncture meridians or lines of flow of Force. They provide the force field matrix—the structural design framework for the growth of the nervous system and other circulatory systems in the human body.

### Field Orientation and Personality Archetypes

These *morphogenetic fields have a specific orientation.* In *plants these may be caused by sunlight—*in *animals and Homo sapiens this is caused by the action of gravity.* The human morphogenetic field will have an overall downward orientation caused by gravity. *Indian yogic and tantric texts spoke at length about the need to reverse this normal field orientation. The evolved being reversed his field orientation from a downward and outward flow to a dynamic model in which the field was aligned upwards towards the brain or the top of the cerebrospinal axis. Such a being was called the "Urdhava Retas" (the one in whose the flow is upwards).* The traditional Hatha yoga exercises physically attempt to invert the field by a system of yogic exercises involving asanas or postures that literally stand the body on its head. The process of evolution, so it appears involves a reversal of field polarity, if one follows the traditional yogic route of a so-called "ascent of the Force (the Kundalini)". To that extent a *"descent of the Super mind" postulated by Aurobindo as the basis of human evolution may be more natural and easier for it takes advantage of the powerful force of gravity.* Perhaps the field orientation is linked to the Jungian personality archetypes—the extrovert and the introvert. The extroverted personality archetype has the field orientation flowing downwards and outwards. The introverted archetype has the current flowing inwards and upwards to form introverted and introspective personalities.

## Autonomous Hierarchies, Holons and the Field Organisations

The morphogenetic field appears to comprise of a loose hierarchy of semi–autonomous "sub-fields" with organ specific functions. These exist as specific sub (or component) programmes within the overall field informational system. The centralised control exercised by the Field brain appears to be marginal and is of a loose or federal nature at best. A lot of autonomy is left for the sub parts. *Arthur Koestler has called these hierarchies of autonomous sub parts "Holons". A complex information system can function only through the agency of a conglomerate of such autonomous, self-regulating hierarchies of sub parts.* This is much like the structure of an army. A corps for example comprises of three divisions. Each of these divisions comprise of three brigades—the brigades of three battalions of a thousand men each. Each battalion is more or less an autonomous part or holon that administers its own internal affairs with minimum external control or directions. It is a specialised orchestra of war in miniscule—a small army—a small microcosm that replicates the essential features of the larger microcosm.

How does this holon concept workout in practice? Let us step back into the field of embryology for a while. A morphogenetic field is the basic blue of life—that contains all the information necessary to programme the basic building blocks of life—the DNA and RNA molecules of our cells. A morphogenetic field by itself cannot produce a physical organism. It has to act upon the single fertilised cell (in the womb) that provides the molecular or cellular basis for the physical organism. The single fertilised cell multiplies by a process of fission into a number of identical cells. After a few weeks the first organ specific zone appear in the foetus. Now each of these cells contain the complete genetic code that will give rise to the whole physical organism—the 6 ft 2" tall wrestler with curly hair and a dimple on the chin. Organ specific zones or morphogenetic zones that have now appeared on the embryo will give rise to the future organs—the heart, lungs, eyes, kidneys etc. *The field acts upon the genetic code of these cells. It sends filter signals that block out all the remainder portion of the genetic code except that which pertains to the specific organ. Thus these particular cells begin to specialise in their specific organ roles.* The process of specialisation is at a cost for it involves "tunnelisation", the blockage of all the remainder, generalist potential. As has been cited earlier, in experiments conducted on salamander embryo, cells were taken from the eye zones of one salamander embryo and grafted on to the belly region of another. They grew an eye lens on its belly! There appears to be a sort of irreversibility about this control or filter process. Once the field has fed the control or filter signals to block the complete genetic output (less the organ functions at the DNA and RNA level)—the signals cannot be reversed.

Is this growth process guided by the foetal brain? Experiments have emphatically proved that this is not so. The foetal brain starts developing alongside the other organ zones. It is only once it is fully formed that it acquires suzerainty over all the other organs (and that this does not happen till near birth). Till then these organ hierarchies grow in an autonomous fashion very much on their own and even later the control of the brain is of a loose or marginal nature. A number of organs—e.g., the heart, lungs, kidneys, liver, and pancreas etc., work automatically on their own without any form of conscious control by the brain. *They are independent hierarchies or holons within the overall hierarchal structure of the body.*

*The morphogenetic field therefore comprises of a number of autonomous, function specific hierarchies or, sub programmes within its informational complex.* These programmes are autonomous and once released act in an irreversible manner.

### Energy–Information Transfer Centres: Step down Transformers

The field permeates the body. There appears to be a one to one cell correspondence between the field and the body. Informational inputs are continually fed from the field to the basic biological "chips"—the hydrocarbon based colloidal chips of the DNA and RNA with their four-letter language code. These self replicating "bio-chips" are a million times more "intelligent" or efficient then the metallic silicon chips of electronics, which work on the binary

(O.1) language of Boolean algebra. In terms of micro-miniaturisation the (VLSI) Very Large Scale or Extremely Large Scale Integrated Circuits (ELSI chips), which have been the bases of the electronic revolution. The application of the mathematical tenets of the information theory was long overdue in the field of living systems. They are vastly complex organisms in which the amount of flow of information is simply phenomenal. To handle this amount of informational flow from the field to the body and vice-versa, it would theoretically be plausible to propose the existence of certain centres, which specialise in massive information transfers. These centres should process raw information and feed it up and down in a processed form. The yogic texts have given elaborate accounts of such "centres" in very great detail. *These have variously been called the charkas—or the wheels, or energy centres. These act as step down transformers that help to convert the field informational input into specific biochemical messages which programme the metabolical functions.* They are co-located with the endocrine or ductless glands that secrete the hormones and regulate our body's metabolism. The endocrine orchestra is set clanging by informational inputs from the field. These transfer centres act as localised bio-computers that regulate the ordered flow of information from and to the field.

These transfer centres exist in the morphogenetic field. In the physical body they are co-located with the endocrine glands and the nerve plexuses that have been described earlier in the book. These classical centres are all located along the cerebro-spinal axon—along the region of the maximum flux density of the force field.

## The Tree Architecture of the Field

The core of the field is centred around the cerebro spinal axon. This theoretically should be the region of the maximum flux density of the force field. The yogic charka theory localised all the energy-transfer centres along this axon. The axon has two poles—the brain that floats on top of the axon and the reproductive region that lies at its base.

*The reproductive cells incidentally are generalist cells. They contain the entire genetic code, unfiltered and unblocked* ready to be transmitted to create future offspring.

*The neurons of the brain have the maximum evolutionary potential. Their position atop the cerebro-spinal axon is UP TO HERE metaphorically indicative of the directional thrust of evolution.* The brain is perhaps the largest and the principal information energy transfer centre. Massive amounts of information inputs from the field are decoded into chemical instructions here; into Neuro-transmitters of varying complexity—simple Amino acid neuro-transmitters, the mono-amine transmitters and the highly complex peptides and polypeptides, which are possibly the basis of learning. The immune system carries out its signalling or information transfer through protein messengers called Lymphokines. Now Neuro-peptides, which influence moods and emotions, fit smugly into receptors of Lymphokines. The Macrophages (white cells) themselves release Neuro-peptides. Peptides therefore play a very important role in information transfer.

The bulk of the signalling, however, is done by the very simple Amino acid neuro-transmitters. The more complex monoamines account for only one percent of the neural traffic (but this is a vital one percent that is responsible for the major psychoses). *The peptides are the most complex of all information structures (they comprise of two or more Amino acids chained together in head to tail links). These entrain the endocrine glands, which secrete the hormones.* Chemically these could be basically proteins and peptides or Aromatic compounds or steroids. In a progression of complexity, the information transfer hierarchy is as over leaf.

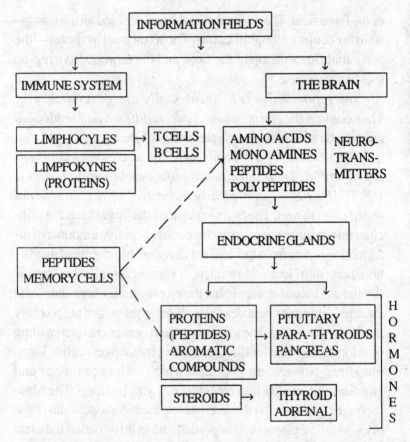

## THE INFORMATION LANGUAGE OF BIOLOGICAL SYSTEMS

Tropic hormones secreted by the master endocrine glands located in the brain entrain or activate the lower endocrine glands. The brain therefore is the chief information processor and targets chemical coded instructions to the other information distribution centres in the body. The peptide molecules therefore stand out as the common language between the Information Field, the Brain and the Immune System. They are the Biochemical equivalents of the Soma that descends.

## Photosynthesis of Field Output

It is time to return once again to the tree or "Kalpavriksha" symbol for clues. This kind of "imagic thinking" can provide us vital insights into the nature of the field. Viewed on the basis of the tree analogy, *each of the billions of neurons in the brain could be regarded as a tiny microprocessor. Each of them basically processes information. Let us visualise the neurons like the leaves of a tree. The leaves soak in the sunshine and carry out photosynthesis that converts the informational energy inputs from the field into the language of Neuro transmitters.* Could the neurons, on the basis of this analogy, soak in the informational energy input and carry out photosynthesis of sorts? A photosynthesis that converts the informational energy inputs from the field into the language of Neuro-transmitter signalling? By day the trees take in carbon dioxide and exude oxygen. By night they reverse the process.

*Could we assume that by day the neurons soak in the field input. By night when we sleep, the neurons transfer the days processed information to the field.* Dreams *represent a process of mental digestion. The brains hologramic images not transferred to the field are played out internally as dreams.* More probably we could speculate about a continual two-way traffic, with overall stress on information receipt by day and processed information transfer to the field by night, while the organism rests.

## States of the Informational System: The Quantum Mechanics of Consciousness

Quite possibly the known states of consciousness, (dreaming, waking and deep sleep—each of which is characterised by a different electrical brain wave pattern) represent the three energy states of the Informational Field-System. Now quantum mechanically each system can exist in a number of possible energy states. It will, by itself, exist in its lowest possible energy state (even as an electron will normally be found in its lowest orbital or energy state). A fourth state of consciousness beyond waking, dreaming, and deep sleep has been theorised about in oriental philosophy. (In Vedantic lore it is called "Turiya"). Possibly this represents the next higher energy state of this Field information system. *By psychosomatic exercises we can "excite" the system so that it jumps to its next state. It cannot stay in that excited state for long and must fall backs to its normal state. In so doing the energy difference between the two states is given off as a "Quanta" or a package of energy.* (The next chapter on meditation will deal in detail with this theory). At this stage we would like to propose that the so-called Kundalini process represents this "Quanta" of energy that is released once we are able to excite our "Field" into its next higher state. It is a specific Quanta—a specific energy packet that equals the potential difference between the two energy states of the system. It acts like the release of an autonomous sub programme, as a Holon. This energy packet translates into an eruption of Neuro-transmitters, and endocrine secretions. It acts not only on the Brain and endocrine system but also upon the Immune system. It is important to understand the analogy we have taken from Einstein's explanation for the phenomenon of Photo electricity (special theory of Relativity). It is explained on page 185 diagrammatically.

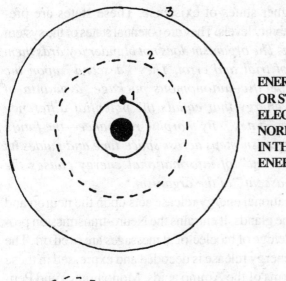

**ENERGY LEVELS OR STATES OF AN ELECTRON. IT NORMALLY EXISTS IN THE LOWEST ENERGY STATE (1)**

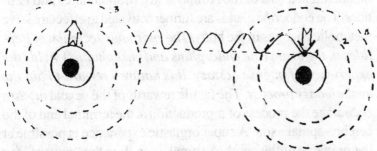

**WHEN EXCITED IT JUMPS TO THE NEXT ENERGY LEVEL (2)**

**WHEN SOURCE OF EXCITATION IS REMOVED, IT FALLS BACK TO ITS ORIGINAL ENERGY STATE (1). DIFFERENCE BETWEEN THE TWO STATES IS GIVEN OFF AS A PACKAGE OR "QUANTA" OF ENERGY.**

## The Kundalini as an Autonomous Sub programme of the Field

The Kundalini is a specific quanta of information—energy that is unleashed upon our systems, once we are able to "excite" it towards its higher states of existence. These states are pre-structured probability levels. They are potential states of the system that exist per se. *The organism does not blunder towards them by a process of trial and error. They "descend" upon the system in a specific–autonomous package, a quanta of informational energy that equals the potential difference between the two states". By morphic resonance—the future shape of the organism steps across space-time and guides its growth. A "descent" of informational energy causes the evolutionary "ascent" of the organism.*

The informational energy release acts upon the neuron and master endocrine glands. It entrains the Neuro-transmission process. A whole deluge of bioelectrical messages are fired off. The informational energy release is decoded and expressed in these biochemical terms of the Amino acids, Monoamines and Peptides. The endocrine glands are further activated to effect massive metabolic changes in the body. *The enormous secretion of Peptides in the brain (the endorphins and enkephalins) yields the experience of intense ecstasy. It is nature's reward to aid the evolutionary process.* The tactile rewards of the sexual orgasm encourage the process of reproduction at the terminal end of the cerebro-spinal axon. A super orgiastic experience is possible at the pinnacle of the cerebro-spinal axon. It is the "reward" for abetting or encouraging evolution to the next energy state of the system.

## Actualisation of Morphogenetic Potentials

The Kundalini phenomenon then represents the actualisation of morphogenetic potentials. These morphogenetic potentials are structured into the field as latent possible states of the system. The system can be excited temporarily to "jump" into these states. As it falls back to its original state, it is rewarded by a quanta of informational energy that is released upon the brain and *acts as an autonomous sub programme, as a Holon. Its action once released is irreversible.* One is just supposed to "surrender" to it. *The Indian Yogic texts are full of the need to "surrender" oneself to this process—even as the process of puberty is irreversible and autonomous. It unleashes itself upon the organism and sets in train the metabolic and hormonal changes that guide the growth and sexual maturation of the organism. The "Kundalini process" brings about even more violent metabolic, physiological and psychological changes.* The experiencing organism becomes a hapless victim. It can only "observe". It cannot assume charge of this process of change. Pandit Gopi Krishna's account brings this out most vividly. An ancient tantric icon represents the Shakti (energy) or Maha Kali dancing naked upon the supine corpse of Shiva (the conscious principle). Perhaps this imagic construct expresses most beautifully the unleashing of a second puberty process that works itself out in a definitive, teleological way that is inexorable and frightening. Where does this action commence—at the terminal pole of consciousness as the Tantras depicted—or in the brain as Aurobindo and my own teacher claimed? An objective analysis seems to indicate that the action is primarily originated in the main transfer centre of the brain. *The Kundalini Quanta of information energy descends upon the neurons and entrains that massive deluge of bio-chemical signalling. Signals that are converted into the "soma flow" of the peptides of ecstasy,* and entrain the classical Nirvana experience; signals that entrain the endocrine orchestra to play a new metabolic symphony; to unleash metabolic changes that mediate a more creative intelligence—that express themselves in enhanced charisma and creativity levels and extra sensory perception abilities based on anomalous phenomena that we do not understand fully as yet.

**The Effects of the Release on Field Orientation:** The quanta of energy release expresses itself through the transfer centre that is most active in the organism. If the given organism is sexually very active, the energy release may be discharged in a bout of hypersexual activity. If the energy flow channels are more accustomed to express themselves through the brain, then it will manifest as enhanced mental creativity. This was the Tantric view. Theoretically, the energy release can occur at any of the seven "charkas" or transfer centres. Habitually it will occur at the centre that is most active i.e., the reproductive centre—hence the Tantric emphasis on the terminal pole of the cerebro-spinal axon. A more enlightened view perhaps would be *that the ancient Tantric philosophers had mistaken "effects" for the "causes". The brain incidentally is the chief sexual organ. Gonad tropic hormones secreted by it alone can trigger the gonads into hyper activity. The main release occurs in the core of our brain. What we witness elsewhere are merely effects of the hyper secretion of Neuro-transmitters and tropic hormones.* The brain neurons relapse into refractory periods after massive dosages of neuro-transmitters. This explains the episodic or cyclothymic nature of the process. *It waxes and wanes. It makes the fire of life glow more brightly, flare up and then fade out in sinusoidal cycles—in crests of excitement and ecstasy and troughs of despair and depleted output.* The inner elixirs wax and wane, till at last the neurons can express a steady stream of evolved consciousness.

## The Immune System and the Self

One of the prime functions of the Immune system is to distinguish self from non-self. It is only based upon this sensing of biological identity that the immune system detects, tags attacks and eliminates an intruding organism. It is therefore one of the underlying components of the biologic identity of self. The immune response serves to define the biologic self. One of the prime tools of the immune system (especially the immunological memory) are the complex Neuro-transmitters called the polypeptides. These play a major role in the learning process in the human brain. There are also the bases of the action of Soma. *The Atharva Veda mentions Soma as the king of all medicines.* (It is the sovereign of all "Aushaddhis"). The action of Soma therefore not only generates ecstasy. It is the key to creativity and order in the psyche. It is the key to all healing for it strengthens the Immune system and ensures longevity of the biological organism. It could therefore reverse/ slow down the aging process.

## Biological Lasers

Another theory has it that the massive release of this *"Quanta of Informational" energy realigns the field. It is inverted and made "Urdhva Retas". It is this perhaps that explains the enhanced "animal-magnetism" of the inverted field. Aligned up or down—the crucial point is that like a magnet—it is all aligned in one direction. Possibly this animal magnetism is the source of charisma.* Possibly the Kundalini energy release erupts like a biological laser in the consciousness. *The hologramic images within the head are then pumped by a powerful biological laser—what such a mind visualises—it actualises.* Perhaps this biological laser phenomenon could be at the root of all Extra Sensory perceptions and Quasi-sensory communications. Telepathy, Clairvoyance, Clairaudience it all could be explained on this theoretical basis. It would be source of all Anomalous phenomena. The activation of a biological laser could lend a strange dynamism to one thoughts and desires. It could also empower our Human Energy Fields to exert influence on other Human Fields and serve to realign them or act as a catalyst for triggering off similar experiences in them. Hence the criticality of the "Guru – disciple" bond in most Eastern mystic lore.

## Kala Agni: The Reversal of the Arrow of Time

Let us now return to our earlier theme of the ascent of the Kala Agni. Meditation causes a revolution in our perception of time. In the frontal lobes of our brain our time sense somehow becomes fused with the energy of our emotions. This energic amalgam of emotion and time is possibly the basic powerhouse of our biological beings. It must perforce be mobilised in any process of our evolution. It is the Vedic Kala Agni. It is the energy of Time that somehow empowers this quantum jump in our consciousness to the next level of probability. These quantum fields of probabilities (these Richas?) exist per se. They are pre-structured levels of our Morphogenetic field. The Kala Agni, the energy of time rises. Our field jumps to this higher quantum level. It cannot stay there forever. It relapses to its original state. The difference between the two energy levels is given off as a Quanta of Energy, as Soma. *Kala Agni rises Soma descends.* The streams of the "Vedic Ratasya dharas" descend to bathe us with ecstasy and euphoria, to charge us with a new creative energy, positivism, optimism and even grandiosity and euphoria. Physiologically we go through a second process of puberty as it were. The descent of Soma is the massive release of peptides and polypeptides, the eruption of Endorphins and Enkephalins in the human brain. These in turn entrain the endocrine glands to secrete the tropic and other hormones that will fuel the new metabolic process of major evolutionary change in the biological organism. These physiological changes are essential to express the evolved higher consciousness. This is where we propose to enlarge Sheldrake's theory of Morphic resonance in terms of the insights provided by the Vedic concept of "Kala Agni", the energy of Time. The rise of the Kala Agni represents a radical reversal of the arrow of time itself. From its inexorable and unidirectional flow from the past, to the present and into a future—it is now reversed dramatically. The biological organism is now no longer pushed by its past inheritance. It now transcends the sphere of information coded in its genes. Its future Morphic potentials reach out to it. They step back quantum mechanically to guide and shape its unfolding in the present. *Where all other biological organisms seek their Morphic resonance from the patterns of the past, the new prophetic organism is focussed upon the future.* It gets its Morphic resonance from the probabilities inherent in its evolutionary future. The rise of the Kala Agni therefore symbolises the reversal of the arrow of time. The Kala Agni rises and the Soma descends with its train of peptides and polypeptides and associated hormones. It causes an upsurge of ecstasy in the biological organism. It unleashes a teleological process of inner unfolding that is more or less autonomous, for it springs from the potential state that is already there in the future. The crucial difference is that unlike all other biological organisms, the source of its Morphic resonance is not located in its past but in the future. It is the future shape and form that step backwards quantum mechanically to bring about an evolution of the organism. Such an organism, in which the Kala Agni has arisen, becomes a Prophetic life form. It anticipates and consciously grows towards its future. It is no longer propelled by its past but pulled by its future. It becomes a visionary being that can forecast and feel the shape of future events and changes. Such a life form therefore is so much better placed to anticipate such changes and ensure their actualisation and implementation in a conscious manner. It does not blunder or stumble towards this evolutionary change. The future probabilities reach out to guide its unfolding in the present. The direction of Morphic resonance has undergone a dramatic shift. As opposed to the inheritance of the past, it has progressed to the lodestar like pull of the future. We actualise the inherent potentials of our own future—we open our arms to receive their aid and enlightenment.

The reversal of the arrow of time is not mere conjecture. It is a scientific fact. Ilya Prigogrine, the Noble prize winning chemist has asserted that the reversal of the arrow of time is possible. The Kundalini phenomenon, the rise of the Kala Agni, reverses the arrow of time and thereby liberates the organism from the push of its past patterns of emergence, to the "Pull" of its future evolutionary potentials.

# CHAPTER THIRTEEN

# MEDITATIONS ON MORPHIC RESONANCE

## Quantum Mechanics and Meditation

*The Kundalini then is an autonomous sub programme—a holon in the human morphogenetic field. In psychological terms it acts as a release of latent genetic potentials. It acts primarily upon the brain as a massive release of informational energy*—an unfolding of the autonomous sub programme. This programme acts upon the neurons of the hypothalamus, the Limbic system and the pituitary and releases massive doses of neuro-peptides, of endorphins and enkephalins and their associated monoamines and amino acid transmitters. *The Rig Vedic Aryans called this flow of Neuro-peptides the flow of Soma. It led to ecstasy, and creativity.* It conferred charisma and phenomenal creative abilities. It led to altered states of consciousness. It led to species evolution.

*The release of Soma or the action of the Kundalini* the coiled one—the latent or potential energy of evolution *was marked by a significant mobilisation of the endocrine orchestra—the neuro-peptides, dopamine and Norepinephrine acted upon the endocrine glands of the brain. The hypothalamus and pituitary in specific were violently stimulated to secrete tropic hormones that set the entire endocrine orchestra clanging.*

Such a total mobilisation of the endocrine system—*such rapid and accelerated growth occurs in the human body in quanta's—in specific episodic spurts.* Two such episodes occur in each human lifetime: —

(a)  Birth: This total mobilization for accelerated growth occurs at the time of conception. It is unleashed upon the zygote—the single fertilized cell in the womb. It creates the foetus and then the newborn baby and continues at this rapid metabolic rate of growth (when Anabolism far outstrips catabolism) till about the first few years of life. Then it appears to slow down and around the $7^{th}$ or $8^{th}$ year of life and seems to go into a period of latency.

(b)  Puberty: At puberty, trigger signals from the hypothalamus set the endocrine orchestra clanging again. Soma tropic and gonad tropic hormones are secreted and activate the lower endocrine glands to secrete the growth of sexual hormones. Specific and significant changes take place in the human organism that makes it sexually active. Male and Female sexual characteristics rapidly arise to establish our sexual identities. The entire process unwinds as an autonomous sub programme that regulates itself; that proceeds apace in the body till it has completed its task of transforming the adolescent into a sexually active and fully grown adult organism.

The common factor in both these phases of rapid or accelerated growth (that actualise rather like a "burst communications" process in electronics) is the fact *that Anabolism far outstrips Catabolism.* This is reflected in the organism. *These episodes of rapid growth and change represent two quantum levels or intrinsic energy states of the organism per se. The growth occurs in "quanta's"—in discontinuous bursts when the pro-*

*cesses of Anabolism or growth rapidly and dramatically out-
pace the processes of catabolism or decay.* In the information
energy sphere then, both these states are quantum levels to which
the organism leaps up as an entity at the specific time in the history
of the Field-body complex. *Indian Vedic and the Tantric or
yogic lore all seem to point out to the existence of a third
Quantum or energy level in the informational energy complex. This points out to the possibility of a Thi*rd *such revolution in the organism (a third quantum jump as it were)* which
mobilises the entire endocrine orchestra and mediates violent
changes in the metabolism rate and the body-mind complex. *This
process was called the "Second Birth". One who had undergone such an inner evolution was called the "Twice Born" or
the Brahmin. His remarkable gifts of creative intelligence,
charisma and phenomenal communication abilities set him
apart from other men.* Such a creative minority of Brahmins or
"twice born" ones (Jedis?) was given the highest place in society
and *charged with providing the ideological leadership and
intellectual guidance to the race.* The "birth" metaphor is very
significant and points to the key role of the endocrine orchestra in
mediating *this very significant process of "a second puberty"
that results in a sublimation of the libido and its re-
channelisation for intellectual or theory making activities of
the brain. This process of mobilisation then was on par with
the other two episodic landmarks in the history of the evolution of the organism—The Birth and puberty upheavals.* Sublimation or what Carl Jung has called "individuation") was its third
quantum level and third manifestation. *It caused as major an
upheaval in the inner environment as the preceding two episodes of birth and puberty.* A rapid influx of energy could excite
the Field per se to "jump" to that higher Quantum level of its
reality. This form of evolution then is not a trial and error or a hit
and miss process. It is not the result of genetic mutations acquired

accidentally in the struggle with a vicious and hostile environment. *The next level already exists per se on the "Deity" model that Samuel Alexander had speculated about in his "Emergent Theory of Evolution".* It is the next higher level of reality or probability that emerges like a lodestar to pull up to itself the struggling matter. It is the next Quantum level of probability that already exists per se and towards which evolution proceeds in a definitive process of growth. Ilya Prigogine has now substantiated the feasibility of movement along both directions of the time continuum i.e., not just from the past, to the present and on to the future but also the reverse—from the Future to the Present. *The Kundalini then, appears to be genetic trigger mechanism— where a relatively simple command or signal releases extremely complex, pre-set action patterns. By this means* the organism is able to reap the full benefits of the autonomous, self-regulating character of its subdivisions—its holons on the lower level. *Such a trigger signal releases preset action patterns, which transform the implicit message into explicit terms—from the general to the particular.* Any energy system can exist in a number of possible energy states or quantum levels. It normally exists in the least or lowest possible energy state. If excited it can jump or leap to the next Quantum level. However, it cannot stay in that excited or higher energy state for long. It slips down to its original energy state and the difference in the two energy states is given off as a quanta (packet) or photon of energy. This analogy from Quantum mechanics should help us to speculate about the nature of the energy transfer from the Informational Energy Field to the body.

## The Topology of Consciousness

The Human Consciousness has three known states, waking, dreaming and deep sleep. These have their characteristic EEG (Electroenchophalograph) Brain wave patterns. The Indian philosophical texts mentioned a fourth State of Consciousness called "Turiyavasta". It was distinct from the normal three states of waking, dreaming and deep sleep.

(a) *The deep Sleep phase* is characterised by Delta and Theta waves from 1-3 to 4-7 cycle per second (cps).
(b) The *dreaming stage* is interspersed with spurts of Beta waves. Alpha waves are 8-13 cps and occur in rest.
(c) Beta waves 13 cps and more represent the *waking stage*.

In recent experiments conducted on subjects practising the meditational technique of TM (Transcendental Meditation) popularised by Maharishi Mahesh Yogi, R K Wallace and Benson have identified a Fourth State of Consciousness characterised by a distinctive Brain wave pattern. It has variously been described as restful awareness—and has a predominance of Alpha Brain waves rhythm (that donate rest) with complete awareness (represented by Beta rhythm).

This Fourth state of Consciousness represents a higher energy state of the Informational Energy Field Complex. By the process of meditation we seem to take the quantum jump to this higher state of consciousness. Could we assume that on the Quantum Analogy we cannot remain in this "excited energy" state for long? The system perforce has to come down to its lower state of energy. In so doing the difference in the two energy levels is released as a Quanta—a packet of informational energy that pulses through our Neurons—that releases a train of neuro-peptides and dopamine and Norepinephrine that sets our endocrine orchestra clanging. That mobilises our metabolism to mediate definitive physiological changes that will help us to make stable that next higher stage of consciousness—which seems to be the target of human evolution.

## Morphic Resonance: The Mechanics of Meditation

Reflection on the Kundalini phenomenon shows it to be an autonomous sub-programme (a Holon) in the informational energy Field. It appears to be the latent genetic potential that is unfolded by trigger signals from the field. What exactly is the nature of the "trigger" that unleashes this informational—energy programme from our morphogenetic field? The release of this programme sets in train the release of neuro-peptides, which in turn activate the endocrine orchestra. *The Kundalini or Soma mechanism is not really that esoteric an agency. It appears to be active in a very general way in surprisingly large segment of our global population. All manifestations of creative activity are part of its domain. It is this mechanism that is unconsciously active in all creative people—in artists, poets, writers, saints and scientists all over the globe. The hallmarks of creative activity are synthesis and integration—simplification and ideology or theory formation, the generation of new ideas.* Clinically creative activity is marked by episodic work spurts and mood swings that seasonally oscillate between grandiosity and euphoria and stark depression. Creative art strays into the realm of abnormal psychology. The manic-depressive or cyclothymic cycle is its hallmark. *The so-called Kundalini phenomenon then is not confined to one single socio-cultural setting. It is a universal phenomenon that is more wide spread than was imagined till now.*

These spontaneous general arousals not withstanding, there is a considerable body of clinical evidence to show that Eastern mystics and savants have consciously unleashed this process in themselves by the psychosomatic exercise of meditation. Meditation that seems to enable us to take the quantum Jump to a Fourth state of consciousness. It is this that serves as the conscious trigger that activates this tract of informational energy in our morphogenetic fields. *What exactly is meditation? How does it work? How does it activate this evolutionary mechanism?* How does it trigger the release of Soma or the Kundalini? How does it kinetise the Kala Agni? A considerable body of research has recently been conducted on meditation and altered states of consciousness. In the main, the techniques of Transcendental meditation taught by Maharishi Mahesh Yogi and Zen meditation techniques of Rinzai and Soto Zen have been the subject of much experimentation. All these experiments have confirmed the onset of a "fourth state of consciousness" with the following physiological correlates.

(a) *Brain wave patterns* of subjects in meditation indicate that they are awake and in a state of restful alertness. Metabolic rate is generally reduced to a level below that of deepest sleep.

(b) *Total oxygen consumption* shows a mean decrease of twenty percent a figure that is greater than the mean decrease for an entire night of sleep.

(c) *Galvanic skin Resistance* (an indicator with an inverse relationship to stress level) increases by a factor of from two to eight. (8 hours of sleep increases this indicator by a factor of two).

(d) *Lactate Ion concentration* was found to decrease over thirty percent during meditation. The increase in Lactic acid accounts for fatigue and in excess for anxiety neurosis.
   Source: (Wallace R K "Physiological Effects of Transcendental Meditation", SCIENCE Vol 167 pp 1751-1754; Mar 27, 1970).

Much the same result has been reported for Zen meditation systems by the Japanese scientists Karamatsu and Hurai (1966) in their EEG investigations of Zen meditators. The results have been comprehensively summarised by A Kishige (1970) and highlight decreased rates of respiration and oxygen consumption, a decrease in spontaneous Galvanic Skin Response (GSR) and slight increase in pulse rate and blood PH. These are the established correlates of meditation—but that still leaves us with the central question of what is meditation? One Western researcher has described meditation as a state of deep passivity, combined with awareness. *Meditation makes possible a state of clear, relaxed awareness, in which the flow of thought is reduced and an attitude of detached observation is maintained. Thoughts are not prevented but are allowed to pass off without elaboration* ("On meditation" by E W Manpin from "Altered States of Consciousness edited by Charles T Tart John Wiley and Sons). There are several different systems of meditation. These involve two basic approaches: —

**(a) The Focussed Deployment of Attention:** This is done usually on a bio-resonator like the sound of breathing (Zen and Theravada Buddhist meditation) or more usually a specified sound structure called the Mantra. (Tantric meditation and Transcendental Meditation both employ this mode). The mantra is a very important concept. *It is a sub-vocal sound, which has been very specifically chosen for the meditator. It is a resonance frequency which seems to correspond some how to his basic "octave" or note.* When the attention is directed or deployed on to this sound structure by sub-vocal repetitions, it seems to set into train a whole chain of bio-resonators. We shall come back to this thesis later and elaborate on this aspect in great detail For the time being, the classical Yoga of Patanjali describes eight steps to meditation. The first five are preparatory and deal with a restrained and moral conduct, control of senses, breathing exercises etc. The last three steps are Dharna (concentration) Dhyana (meditation) and Samadhi (The Transcendental or Fourth State). *Thus concentration or sharply focussed attention is the first* *essential step that leads to meditation. Attention is given an internal focus on the sub-vocal sound structure.* This concentration or controlled deployment of attention is not a forced process or a struggle. One does not wage war to quell the rise of discordant or distracting thoughts, abstractions and fantasies. Rather one lets them come and gently pass and goes back to the internal focus on the sub-vocal sound structure of the Mantra. Over a period of time this single point of attention also seems to fade away and *there are prolonged patches of pure passivity in which there is neither thought nor mantra. That is meditation. Concentration however is an essential preliminary exercise. That is why this phenomenon is so widespread, for artistic, scientific or any form of creative activity needs high levels of concentration. And prolonged habits of concentration make us slip unconsciously into these meditative reveries that presage the on set of the Fourth state of consciousness in our personal evolution.*

**(b) The Expansion of Attention:** This is the alternative path to meditation. The meditator attempts to attain a state of maximum receptivity to internal and external stimuli. This is the path of Soto Zen and in a way of Jiddu Krishnamurthy. Dr. Paul Brunton has also left descriptions of this process of inducing passivity or "inner watchfulness" of the states of thought and being. Patanjali's classical Yoga Sutras state, "Yoga is preventing the mind stuff (Chitta) from assuming the modification of thought vortices (Vrittis)". "The basic goal of both approaches to meditation is to gain control over attention deployment in an effort to develop *an awareness that allows every stimulus to enter into consciousness devoid of our normal selection process and automatic categorising: devoid of normal tuning and input selection"* (Norango and Ornstein 1971). This was succinctly expressed by Patanjali as a *cessation of "Sankalpa-Vikalpa"*—the formative response of acceptance or rejection; the habitual tossing of the mind, the formation of mental acts of will and volition.

## One Practical Technique of Meditation

There are several hundred different techniques of meditation. To bring the discussion from the theoretical to the practical level I shall briefly describe the meditation technique, which was taught to me by my learned teacher, Swami Pranavananda Saraswati, easily one of the greatest living exponents of the art of deep meditation in our times. The process of meditation is easy to induce if we follow a set routine that habituates our system to automatically slip into meditative states at the appointed time. Meditation is best done in the cool parts of the day (at the junctions of day and night i.e. at dawn and dusk). If possible one should have a quiet meditation room set aside for the purpose. For meditation one sits in the classical Lotus or half Lotus posture (Padma or Siddha Asan). In this the knees and buttocks form a stable—three-cornered base. It is important that one keeps the spinal column and head erect (otherwise there is a tendency to slip into drowsiness or stupor and mistake that for meditative states). One assumes the posture and gazes steadily in front to a point on the wall that is level with the eyes. Then gradually one lowers the gaze to the floor ahead of ones knees and in so doing closes the eyes. *How one closes the eyes is important—for it avoids unnatural cross-eyed stances that tire the eye muscles.* The meditation process is like this: —

(a)  Watch your breathing. Do not consciously manipulate its rate. Just observe how your breath goes in and out of your nostrils. Watch it in a gentle and detached manner. Every moment of our lives we are drawing in and drawing out our breath but we are never consciously aware of its sound—the eternal sound of breath. Focus on this sound.

(b) As you draw in your breath mentally recite the sound "So". As you exhale mentally recite the sound "Ham". Let this intonation superimpose it self on the sound of your breathing— "So" as you inhale and "Ham" as you exhale.

(c) Various thoughts will arise, abstractions and fantasies will clamour around in your head. Gently let them pass. DO NOT fight or struggle to suppress your thoughts. Such an effort is tiring and counter productive. It only succeeds in raising more thoughts. Gently get back to that sub vocal chant—that is in step with the rhythm of your breath. Remember the slogan "Thoughts may come and thoughts may go but the breathing goes on for ever".

(d) As you meditate your breathing will become shallower and also become less numerous. You will get occasional snatches when there is no breathing (mantra) and there are no thoughts. Lengthen out such Shangrilian moments of inner peace. They represent the actual meditative state.

(e) Meditate for 15 minutes a day morning and evening to begin with. Do not get up abruptly and suddenly from meditation. Do it in a languid and unhurried fashion. Do make it a point to evacuate your bladder and bowels before and after the exercise of meditation. A light diet, high in milk and fruit, does seem to help.

## The Action of Resonators in Meditation

Let us now follow the train of Neuro-physiological events that are set off once we commence the process of meditation. We shall primarily be concentrating on the "Focussed deployment of attention", approach based on the meditation technique outlined above. *Itzhak Bentov, an American researcher on the Kundalini used a ballisto-cardiogram, to observe subjects engaged in deep meditation. He observed the onset of a rhythmic sine wave pattern. He attributed this to the development during the course of meditation of a "standing wave" in the aorta—the main artery from the heart. This is reflected in a rhythmic rocking motion in the upper half of the body. This resonating oscillator—the heart aorta system in turn entrains further bio-oscillators, the brain, the cerebral ventricles and the sensory cortex of the brain—which together effect a modification of the cerebral magnetic field.* This coordinated system activates a travelling stimulus, an oscillating current in the sensory cortex tissue, which is finally polarised to a point *where each hemisphere of the brain produces a pulsating magnetic field.* In fact Bentov states that the heart-aorta complex contributes a primary resonating oscillator driving four-associated micro-oscillators. When locked into the heart-aorta resonating system, the combined operation of these resonating oscillators generates a fluctuating magnetic field around the head.

Because the head is a dense, tight structure, acoustic plane waves generated by oscillations in the body subject the brain to mild rhythmic up and down inputs. *Since the brain tissue acts like piezoelectric gel, these mechanical vibrations can be converted into electrical signals and vice-versa.* This has a stimulating effect, which is further enhanced by vibrations reflected off the skull. *This focuses them on the third and lateral ventricle in the centre of the brain.* They are continuous with the cavity running down the middle of the spinal cord. The cerebro-spinal fluid is set into oscillation by the acoustic plane waves. This produces a second standing wave, this time in the head. *It is these standing waves in the cerebral ventricles that trigger off the circular motion of nerve impulses in the sensory areas of the cortex. The circular movements include at least two of the pleasure centres in the brain,* a fact, which Bentov felt accounted for the tranquillity and happiness felt by the meditators. The sounds heard would be secondary results of standing waves in the cerebral ventricles, activating structures in the middle ear and producing "inner sounds". (Source: Itzhak Bentov: Stalking the wild pendulum—Bentov in Lee Sanella—"Kundalini Psychosis, or Transcendence).

The above description of the meditative process provides us a powerful insight with the real basis of its functioning. *The key is the resonance set in motion by the various bio-resonators. In this system of meditation the focus itself is on the bio-resonator of the breath.* Attention focussed on the constant sound of breathing has a powerful effect that entrains the bio-oscillator of the heart-aorta system. This can clearly be experienced subjectively—the heart seems to pound and the entire spinal column and head rock and sway in a gentle rhythmic motion. This bio-oscillator entrains further bio-oscillators, the brain, the cerebral cortex and the cerebral ventricles. *The cerebral ventricles are the most important regions of the brain (the realm of the Chida kasha—the void of "consciousness").* There are four such ventricles, the Right and the left ventricles below the corpus callosum and third ventricle that lies at their base between the Thalami. It is connected via the sub-arachnoid space to the Fourth ventricle in the Brain Stem. *The Fourth ventricle* lays betweens the cerebellum and medulla in the brain stem—the reptilian core of the brain. *This is the region of the reticular formation—which is supposed to be the seat of human consciousness.* Though located in the ancient and lowly region of the brain, this is a complex relay or switching station that retargets the stimuli being received from the body to various points in the brain. The sensory nerves route branch lines through the reticular formation. Many of its nerve cells supply the Hypothalamus, corpus striatum, cerebellum and different regions of the cerebral cortex. Various kinds of stimuli fed in to the brain start the reticular formation firing signals at targets all around the brain—measurably altering electrical impulses from the cerebral cortex and arousing this so called higher centre. (The cerebral cortex without the reticular formation to drive it is like a great computer without power supply). Without the reticular formation's alerting signals, the brain grows sleepy. It is the "watch dog" in us that stays awake when we sleep and seems to warn us of danger. Damage to this arousing mechanism can cause unconsciousness. Irreversible damage produces coma and sometimes death.

Incidentally the Brain stem also controls important functions like respiration—breathing in and breathing out. *Focussed attention on this bio-resonator puts us in direct contact with the Reticular formation—the royal seat of human consciousness.* The "Soham" mantra, which matches the sound of breathing, literally means, "I am He" or "I am That". *Indeed the "I" is localised in our reticular formations—the seat of our consciousness.* The setting up of bio-oscillators in the brain ventricles—especially the Fourth ventricle, directly effects consciousness by acting upon the Reticular formation—the seat of human consciousness. *Breathing is controlled by the brain stem. Hence the Yogic observation that control of breathing directly and dramatically effects our consciousness is borne out by physiological fact.* The setting up of such bio-resonance in the Fourth ventricle directly acts upon our reticular formation and brain stem and so should help to produce the altered states of consciousness.

**Resonance in the Third Ventricle:** This is located in the region of the Thalami. *Bio-resonance in this resonating cavity directly and profoundly affects the Hypothalamus and pituitary glands and also the pineal gland. These three constitute the core of the endocrine orchestra.* The effects of resonance on these structures can be dramatic and could easily explain the onset of frantic signalling by these master glands.

*The human brain then has four resonating cavities buried deep within its structure. These are the four ventricles of the brain.* The Third ventricle directly affects the Hypothalamus-Pituitary-Pineal complex. The Fourth Ventricle is co-located with the Reticular Formation in the brain stem—the seat of human consciousness—the central switching board for all brain signals. Any altered states of consciousness can only be produced by directly acting upon the Reticular Formation—the seat of consciousness. This appears to be the "silent witness" in us the watchdog that stays alert even when we sleep or dream.

## Bio Resonance—To Morphic Resonance

If we were to build a simple mechanistic picture of the process of meditation and propose a Neuro-physiological explanation for the Soma or Kundalini Phenomena, we could stop right here. The Newtonian world machine model would triumph. Meditation would seem as a deliberate psychosomatic exercise designed to set in train bio-oscillators in the human brain. The brain has four resonating cavities in the ventricles. Resonance in these could powerfully affect the controlling structures of the endocrine orchestra (the Third Ventricle) and in the Fourth Ventricle; it would directly and strongly act upon the seat of consciousness itself— the reticular formation in the brain stem (The reptilian core of the human brain) to produce altered states of consciousness. Breathing is controlled by the brain stem sub-consciously. Hence a reverse or conscious focus on breathing could affect the brain stem, which in turn contains the reticular formation or the seat of human consciousness. We now see the Neuro-physiological basis for the Yogic claims of consciousness having a direct effect upon breathing and vice-versa. We have already explained how many of the physiological correlates of the so called Kundalini process can be easily traced to the massive flow of neuro-peptides, and allied mono-amines transmitters like Dopamine, Serotonin, Epinephrine and Noradrenaline. The consequent increased production of hormones could easily explain the violent upsurges in metabolic activity; the violent pangs of hunger and lust; the emotional male-storms and burning sensations. *The chemical degradation of neuron-receptors, their slipping- into a desensitised or refractory-phase could explain the "depression half" of the manic depressive cycle. A sudden outflow of energy from the core of consciousness shoots up to the core of our physiological functioning—the central processor unit of our endocrine system in the Hypothalamus-Pituitary-Pineal combine.* It results in a lava like eruption of neuro-peptides and their allied train of mono-amine and simple amino acid neurotransmitters. This flow activates the Hypothalamus and pituitary master gland to *commence heavy secretion of tropic hormones that activate the lower endocrine glands.* The neurons however cannot stand this eruption of endorphin and enkephalin peptides for long. *Their receptors get chemically degraded.* The bursts of energy, euphoria and ecstasy pales away. It gives way to exhaustion and depression. Hence the cyclothymic or the cyclic onset of mania followed by depression. But that is just half the picture. What is unleashed is not a random eruption that could target any arbitrary set of neurons. The reticular formation is acted upon and shoots out messages as per a very specific and individual programme—an autonomous programme that unfolds itself in an intelligent and teleological fashion. It seems to be consciously working for a pre-set goal. *It is a goal directed programme—not an erratic and random process of hit and trial.* The vast flow of information cannot be explained by the simplistic mechanistic model. That only gives us a picture of the resultant process—and effects not the causes.

The cause lies in the Field. The informational energy complex descends as a "Quanta" from the Informational Energy Field. It triggers off a massive release of signals from the Reticular formation—the seat of consciousness. These activate the neurons to secrete the neuro-peptides; these activate the Hypothalamic-Pituitary-Pineal core to secrete a lava of Hormones. The inner geysers of delight hit the optic centre to produce a blaze—an ocean as it were—of internal light. The trigger is resonance. The bio-resonance that is set up in the resonating cavities of the brain unleashes a process of Morphic resonance. Not only can shapes step across the past in the space-time continuum but also from the Future. The deity model—the next Quantum level that already exists, descends as a completed programme from the Field core of consciousness. Altered states of consciousness represent the Quantum levels of possibilities in the states of consciousness. Bio-resonance induced by the process of modification triggers off Morphic resonance in the morphogenetic field. The probability structure, the next quantum level already inbuilt into the field, steps out across the space-time continuum. *Formative causation takes hold of the organism. This time it is impelled not by the past but by the probabilities that lurk in the future. It acts upon the organism and guides its future form and structure in an intelligent and teleological fashion. Morphic* resonance is initiated not by the past but by the quantum probabilities that are already a part of its future.

The future structure of the field already exists as quantum waves of probability; as possible states of the energy system. Since space-time itself is a function of the field, *the probability wave can (quantum mechanically) step across both from the past as well as the future. It is a push-pull type of a system, which is not only pushed by the past but also equally pulled by the future.* Mobility in the space-time continuum cannot be restricted to a one-way traffic, from the past to the present and into the future. In a dynamic system, formative causation could well cause the future probable shape to step across and guide growth in the present. This movement in the reverse direction has been highlighted by the works of the Nobel Prize laureate Ilya Prigogrine.

The Vedas have given us an insight into this dramatic reversal of the arrow of time in their concept of the Kala Agni. Meditation causes the Kala Agni to rise. That reverses the arrow of tim

That presses us from the propulsion of our past patterns and fixes us upon our future probabilities. Morphic resonance occurs again— the critical difference is that this time it is not initiated by our Past but triggered by our Future. The Kala Agni ascends; the Soma descends as an autonomous Holon, as a complete Field programme, as a complex cascade of processes and events set in motion by a simple trigger activity—the act of Meditation.

# CHAPTER FOURTEEN

# THE PHILOSOPHY OF EVOLUTIONARY DESCENT: THE IMPLICATE AND THE EXPLICATE ORDERS

## The Concept of Evolutionary Descent

Aurobindo was a stellar landmark in the recent history of intellectual synthesis. A creative scholar par excellence, he was at once a fiery revolutionary who metamorphosed into a sage. In a lifetime of incredible creative work, he did much *to synthesise modern science and Western philosophy. His concept of the "descent of the Super Mind" was a brilliantly original formulation that represented a decisive break from the classical Indian tradition of an evolutionary "ascent of the Kundalini or the Creative Force".* Aurobindo was an intellectual giant—a living modern embodiment of the ancient Indian tradition of "Rishis" or creative seers—the synthesisers of diverse fields of thought—(what Marowitz has called the "Lumpers" as opposed to the "Splitters").

*"Aurobindo's monumental works represent a multi-layered synthesis of the Darwinian Concept of Evolution with ancient Indian systems of thought.* And within the Indian philosophical systems, he affected *a unique synthesis between the Vedic (Nigama) and Tantric (Agama) schools.* He propagated a "descent of the Super Mind" that would bring about an "ascent"

of the human consciousness—A transformation that would bring about a new "Nietzchean breed of superman".

**Directions in the Topology of Human Consciousness:** The terms "ascent" or "descent" are relative and depend upon our standpoint of observation. In the absence of a universal frame of reference, "up" and "down" are merely categories of the measuring consciousness. In the topology of human consciousness these terms are irrelevant.

*Whether human evolution occurs by an "ascent of the Kundalini or a descent of the Super Mind" the significant point to note is that both these views point to a "teleological" or "goal directed" concept of evolution.* From this viewpoint, evolution is not random and erratic; it is not a ruthless process of the survival of the fittest. *It is not "pushed" by the past but represents a view that is "pulled" by the Future.* Our present paradigms are curiously restrictive. They envision time as a strictly one-way street. Motion along it is possible only in one singular direction—from the past to the present and into the Future. Such a deterministic view of time that negates the possibility of movement in the opposite direction is restrictive and (in the light of Einstein's theories of relativity), somewhat inaccurate. Our universal paradigms are structured entirely on the basis of this singular motion property of time.

The new field theories of life are challenging this view of time. Sheldrake's phenomenon of morphic resonance holds out the possibility of the Future shapes or probabilities equally reaching out to the present so as to actualise themselves. I personally had wrestled with this directional conundrum for many years. Does the Kundalini energy rise up as mentioned by the Tantras or does it descend as the super mind, as described by Sri Aurobindo? It does both. The answer is clearly highlighted in the Vedas. The Kala Agni—(the energy of time) rises. It is kinetised and reverses the arrow of time. In response, the Quantas and streams of Soma descend upon the human organism. The deluge of polypeptides creates a revolution in our psyche and leads the physical organism to its next evolutionary stage of development.

The entire conundrum falls easily into place, the confusion of direction is easily resolved when we turn to the Vedas for insights.

The Tantras exclusive focus and certitude about a phenomenal rise or ascent of the Creative energy from the root of the spine to the summit of the brain is not found in the Vedas. They seem to deal with a much more generalised process. The Vedas talk of a rise of the Kala Agni that leads to a descent of Soma. The entire riddle is now so elegantly resolved. It is the Kala Agni that rises to cause a revolution in our perception of Time. It focuses us upon the future. It is the Soma that descends (as streams of truth and ecstasy). Soma entrains a deluge of somatic neurotransmitters and hormones in our biologic beings. It is the king of all medicines. Its peptides strengthen our Immune system and enhance our learning capabilities. The endorphins and enkephalins inundate us with ecstasy. This marks the onset of our inner evolution.

## Schrödinger's Wave Equations and the Universe of Possibilities

In Quantum Mechanics, Schrödinger's wave equation gives us the possibilities that could happen once we make an observation or measurement of any closed system. If we square the amplitude of the wave function we get the probability function. (Possibility as Gary Zukov tells us is not the same as Probability—it is possible that snow can fall in summer—but not probable—except in the Antarctic). The moment we observe a system we exercise a conscious choice as it were. Our perceiving consciousness acts as a filter or gate. All the several "possibility waves" experience a "quantum collapse" and only one possibility is actualised. We choose from the realm of limitless possibilities—one particular possibility. The moment we exercise the choice by making the observation, the probability of all other possibilities become zero except the one that become "one" and actualises. *Hisenberg therefore theorised about a strange kind of physical reality just in the middle between possibility and reality.*

### Rit and Satya

**Rit:** The Vedas offer a fascinating insight into this field of a quantum soup of probabilities. The Vedas mention "Rit" as a condition in which a substance exists without a defined centre. It lurks as a wave of probability in that quantum soup of probabilities. It exists in the info sphere as a tendency to exist, as an archetypal concept. It constitutes the field of probability around which an actual object could be built up subsequently on the plane of matter.

**Satya** on the other hand is defined by the Vedas as a manifest condition in which a centre appears—a Kendra—a seed point for crystallisation, a locus for actualisation arises. The probability waves that are lurking in the infosphere already—now bear down upon this centre or seed point of crystallisation. This core enables them to actualise and emerge into the Truth of their existence. The object materialises and is called Satya. It has emerged into the Truth of our perception and experience. Interestingly, the Vedas state that only when Agni and Soma unite is Satya born. Agni represents the forces of expansion and entropy, Soma that of contraction gravity and attraction. Their constructive balance alone creates actualisation of forms.

Hisenberg's Quantum soup of Probabilities is the basic battleground in the interpretation of Quantum mechanics today. There is the classical Copenhagen interpretation and the more startling

"Many Worlds Interpretation" of Everett Wheeler and Graham. They have theorised that it is possible that in other mutually exclusive dimensions the other possibilities that we have rejected in the act of perception/observation (collapsed Quantum mechanically) may actualise or be seen through to their ultimate conclusions.

On the philosophical plane therefore, if we theorise about a Quantum Field of All Possibilities (a ground state of the Universe)—the observing consciousness acts as a gate or filter which permits one set of possibilities to actualise at a time and be played out from the magma of this ground state.

## Karma

We look into that field of infinite possibilities. What actualise out of them *is determined purely by "chance" as per Quantum mechanics. Eastern philosophy replaces chance by "Karma". The dynamism of past actions and mentations, the patterns of the post shape the geometry of the space time continuum and determine which particular possibility will actualise at what particular point in time.* As per this theory the forces that shape the present are two-way systems. Like a "push-pull amplifier" they are pushed by the past and equally pulled by the future probabilities that are seeking to actualise themselves. All minds are dynamic entities that significantly alter the geometry of the space—time continuum by the very process of mentation. This altered geometry produces the "fault lines" and contours that will shape the future flow of events. These mind generated fault lines in our space-time geometry possibly cause the Kendra's or centres of "Satya" to arise. This forms the locus of materialisation. The Quantum probability is now transformed into reality—it becomes Satya—the truth. For the condition of such materialisation to be ripe, the opposing forces of Agni and Soma have to be in perfect balance. The forces of Agni are expansive centrifugal and entropic.

Soma is the cause of all attractions, cohering and gravitation. Only when these forces acquire a balance, can a concrete object or shape be formed.

## The Implicate Order

This is where David Bhom's theory of the Implicate order comes to our rescue and provides us the philosophical basis that will help us to effect a full fledged synthesis between Eastern mysticism and modern science. Many people regard Bhom as the true disciple of Einstein. Bhom's theory comes startlingly close to the Buddhist concept of the great "Void", or the Shunyata; the Void that holds everything within its stark emptiness as the un-manifest. It is so to speak, the unexpressed or the un-manifest state of the universe. It is the paradoxical nihil, the ultimate ground state of the cosmos that holds everything in its latent or unexpressed form. Some scientists refer to it as the "vacuum" state. It contains all that there was, is or will be within its voidness in the unexpressed (Avyakta) or implicate stage. From this implicate order things become "explicate" and express themselves in the universe that we see around us. What we see does not exhaust even a tiny fraction of that inexhaustible infinity. Everything descends from that Implicate order. The basic difference between Hindu and Buddhist schools of philosophy concerns itself about the nature of the "implicate or the ground state of the universe". The Buddhists experienced it as the utter void, the ultimate nihilistic paradox of the Vacuum state that contains everything. The Hindu Vedantic philosophers on the other hand, described their existentialist experience of this ground state as "Sat-Chit-Amanda"—"Reality-Consciousness-Ecstasy". To them, the ultimate state was not an utter cipher; it was suffused with an overwhelming feeling of Reality, an all encompassing awareness, and incredible Ecstasy. They faulted the Buddhist sages for the imperfection of their "Samadhi" or highest meditative state, which resulted in a flawed experience. They felt the Buddhists had slipped into the "trance-sleep" or the "Jedi Samadhi", hence their nihilistic experience.

*In the Hindu paradigm, consciousness is the ultimate ground state of the universe. The distinction between organic and inorganic is fallacious. Consciousness is the ultimate basis. It is really the implicate order that contains everything within itself in the latent or un-manifest condition of the highest synthesis.* The manifest universe itself is a play or outpouring of this basic stuff of the cosmos. The universe is structured in consciousness. Manifest or un-manifest; Implicate or Explicate are merely the states of this basic stuff of consciousness. Consciousness is thus the basic ground state of the universe; it represents the state of maximum synthesis, and order and coherence. Consciousness is within us, consciousness pervades without. Therefore within the core of consciousness within our brains, is the ground state of maximum order and synthesis. It is this that we touch when we sink inwards in the depths of our meditations. This is the nuclear core of creativity in our beings. It is the core of aliveness, not the emptiness of the ultimate nihil. Both Hindu and Buddhist philosophers however, are agreed on the baffling paradoxical nature of this ultimate ground state. It cannot be expressed in words; it can only be experienced directly. The Vedas state that when we shut off the sensory input into the brain it is left free to experience pure consciousness itself. That is what happens in meditation. We sink inwards till we touch the hologramic core of our consciousness that is indestructible. We encounter the hologramic thumb shaped Agni—the flame that goes from life to life. This pure consciousness within is a drop in the ocean of consciousness without. It is much more. The relationship between the Atman and Brahman is hologramic. It is the same 'one' that has become the 'many'. We touch the core within and paradoxically we experience an incredible wideness of being. We feel ourselves

one with infinity. We also experience an indescribable ecstasy—
we taste Soma. We touch the truth and we reach immortality. We
have touched the ground state of the universe. We have experienced consciousness itself.

## The Spectrum of Cosmic Expression

So we have a theoretical ultimate or ground state—an implicate
order which contains all the infinite possibilities in itself in the latent
stage. Possibly these are densely packed hologramic images that
exist as "Vrittis" or tendencies to exist; as Richas as it were. They
are probability waves that are forever seeking to actualise
themselves. The Eastern theories of evolution then describe a
descent from this latent or un-manifest stage to the manifest or
expressed stage; from the Implicate to the Explicate—(From the
Avyakta to the Vyakta). We can theoretically trace out a continuum
of this descent. It could be expressed as follows: —

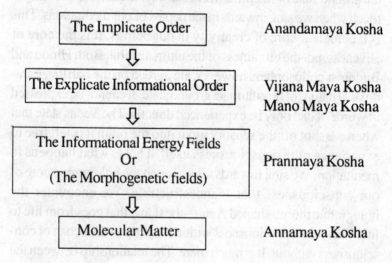

| The Implicate Order | Anandamaya Kosha |
|---|---|
| The Explicate Informational Order | Vijana Maya Kosha<br>Mano Maya Kosha |
| The Informational Energy Fields<br>Or<br>(The Morphogenetic fields) | Pranmaya Kosha |
| Molecular Matter | Annamaya Kosha |

To analyse the so-called spectrum of cosmic expression from the
Implicate to the Explicate order at its lowest Molecular level of

matter, we will have to speculate about *two imperial cosmic impulses—the Entropic impulse that seeks to breakdown all form and order—that destroys and sweeps away the old; and an opposite creative impulse that is forever seeking to create new form and order,* that is forever seeking to express higher and higher orders of intelligence. Both these cosmic impulses act in constructive opposition to one another.

The Entropic impulse forever sweeps away the old. Only thus can continual creation be made possible.

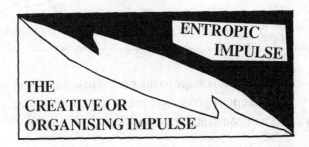

Proceeding by the ancient process of imagic thinking let us superimpose this image on the image of the cosmic spectrum of expression.

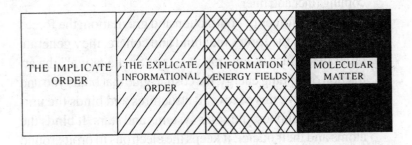

The resultant thought image would become as sketched below: —

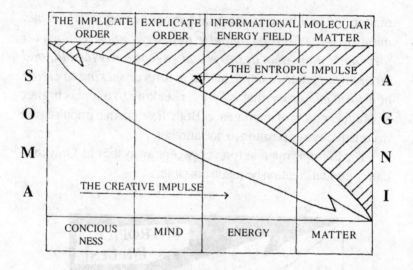

Let us return at this stage to the primal insights of the Vedas. The Vedic concept of physics is premised upon two universal forces that act in constructive opposition to one another.

These are: —

(a) **Agni:** The forces of expansion and entropy—the massive forces of the cosmic big bang, the *centripetal* forces, the impulse towards expansion, towards spreading out and becoming finer and finer.

(b) **Soma:** The forces of contraction and gravitation, the forces of attraction the forces that bind and cohere, they generate order in the face of entropy. It is the "Sneha tatwa", the attraction or binding energy, the cosmic glue that binds you and me in emotive ties of love. It structures and binds the universe, the galaxies, the solar systems and stars. It binds the atoms and their nuclei; it keeps the electrons in orbit around the nuclei of the atoms.

A Chinese proverb says "a picture is worth a thousand words". The pictorial model depicted should help us exercise such an economy of words. Let us now take up each band of the cosmic spectrum in some detail.

**The Implicate Order:** This is the ultimate ground or vacuum state of the universe. It is the field of all possibilities. It contains all the informational order within itself in an un-manifest or implicate condition. It is a super paradoxical state—so akin to the ultimate Buddhistic "Nihil": The Shunyata—the great Void—that is pregnant with limitless possibilities. All the waves of possibilities are contained in this super vacuum state—in a strange, un-manifest manner. It is the ultimate "black hole" that swallows everything in its maw of oblivion and is yet the greatest Cosmic "Quasar" out of which everything emerges. Here Entropy is zero and the creative impulse is at its strongest. The forces of Soma and gravitation are at their peak here.

**The Explicate Informational Order**

The Implicate becomes the Explicate. The Un-manifest becomes the Explicate manifest—the latent actualises itself; the potential becomes Kinetic. The cosmic ground state becomes explicate as the Grand Informational order—the supernal order of intelligence that is evident behind each facet of the cosmos both at the macro and micro levels—The stupendous organisation of the galactic systems, the quasars, pulsars and black holes. The laws with cosmological sweep operate here and govern the macro issues of the universe. They also govern the tremendous intelligence and organisation that is evident at the subatomic and molecular levels. The Implicate order would express itself initially as a vast and awesome order of Information—limitless, boundless, and astounding. Its sheer majesty and scale leaves us speechless with awe. *Aurobindo had called it the Vijnanmay Kosha or the Super Mind. The Vedas called it the Hiranya Garbha or the Universal Mind.* What was latent and un-manifest in the implicate order has now expressed itself as the information and intelligence behind the observed universe. The Creative Impulse is still at its peak but Entropy has made a weak appearance here at this level.

The Informational Energy Fields: From pure information and intelligence we descend to the order of information-Energy. These are the Morphogenetic fields that lie behind all forms and shapes and clusters that animate all organic structures. The pure creative impulse has diluted somewhat. Entropy has made itself felt in a big way. This was possibly the "Pranmaya Kosha" or the vital body of Indian philosophy.

The Molecular Matter: This is reality as we experience it at our day-to-day level. Entropy is the ruling deity in this field of matter. Forms and shapes have to struggle to preserve themselves against its imperious destructive urges. So strong is Entropy at this level—that it is worshipped as the sole reality. Its imperious strength at this level makes us forget the marvellous creative forces that still manage to express themselves in so many wonderful forms—in such a network of symbiotic relationships and cosmic interconnections. The larger the structure; the bigger the cluster, the more vulnerable it is to the ravages of the Entropic forces that are forever seeking to maximise randomness and reduce order (at the molecular level). Agni and entropy are at their peak of power at this level of manifestation. And in a strange, paradoxical way—the field of maximum disorder should give the greatest play to the creative forces—for it rapidly sets aside old forms and worn out structures and compels the creation of newer form and structures. It is the cosmic screen of expression—the state that is continually wiped clean so that fresh creation can proceed apace.

Proceeding ahead with imagic thinking we can now roll the thought diagram of the cosmic spectrum into a cylinder like this (on the origami paper folding Analogy).

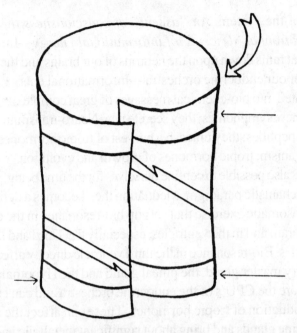

There is a paradoxical point at which maximum entropy overlaps with maximum order and the world of molecular matter in a strange way touches the implicate order itself. Beyond that point, reason and speculation fall like wounded birds from dizzy heights. Agni and Soma unite and Satya is born.

Leaving aside these philosophical flights of fancy, let us return to our original theme. *Evolution is not a random process. It is a teleological and goal directed process. In the Quantum Field of possibilities that lies beyond our dimension, lurk the probable forms that are seeking to express themselves.* They people that fantastic landscape of the universal mind that is densely packed with hologramic images. What is to be already exists as a wave of possibility, as Rita. It exists as the manifold quantum levels where the electron of an atom could exist. If the system is excited, it jumps or ascends to those higher levels or energy states. In its return it takes back a quanta of informational energy of greater order and intelligence to that lower level or (orbital) or energy state of the system. *An "ascent" of consciousness therefore results from a "descent" of informational energy*—Information that rains down upon the neurons of our brains and the structures of our endocrine orchestra—Informational energy that is translated into bio-chemical messages of great complexity. They strike new symphonies; they secrete new Neuro-transmitters and neuro-peptides; they unleash a harvest of tropic hormones upon the organism; tropic hormones of growth and evolution.

It is also possible to confine ourselves for the time being, within the mechanistic paradigm. Meditation then becomes a definitive psychosomatic exercise that sets up bio-resonance in the cortex of the brain and in the ventricles, especially the Third and Fourth ventricles. Bio-resonance in the third ventricle directly affects the Pituitary master gland, the pineal gland and the Hypothalamus. These are the CPU's of the endocrine orchestra and can entrain the production of tropic hormones. These can affect the lower endocrine glands and bring about significant metabolic and hormonal changes in the body. Bio-resonance in the fourth brain ventricle directly affects the Reticular Formation—the Seat of consciousness in the brain. It is this that brings about Quantum jumps in our states of Consciousness. Meditational Exercises affect the Reticular formation and engender altered states of consciousness. It is from this point onwards that we reach the border between the body and the field phenomena between particle Physics and Field Physics—between today and tomorrow.

# EPILOGUE

## DEPTH ECOLOGY: WORSHIPPER OF THE COSMIC FIELD:

### THE FUTURE OF RELEGION

In conclusion then, the four main imagic concepts outlined in this book are the Savitur or the Shining Sun of Intelligence; the Kala Agni or the Fire of Time, Soma, the Elixir of Ecstasy and the Mythical Kalpavriksha Tree—the tree of Life itself. Incidentally, these symbols are the leitmotifs that occur again and again in the Atharva Veda. The Atharva Veda is the last of the Vedas. It stands apart as a unique collection of some 731 hymns and 6000 verses that deal with the deeply mystical science of "Brahma Vidya"— the Science of Consciousness. *In the Atharva Veda, the renowned seer Shaunak asks the great sage Angira "Lord which is that science having known which all else is known?" "That Science", replied sage Angira "is Brahma Vidya"— the science of consciousness. Having known that all else is known".* And as to the nature of this Brahman itself, Angira explained, "Just like the spider throws out and retracts its web; just like herbs and plants and shrubs spring forth from this earth; Just as nails and hair grow from the bodies of living men; so does the universe spring forth from the un-decaying one (from Brahman)".

The highest science therefore is the Science of Consciousness. Today the science of Physics has undergone a revolutionary transformation. The certainties of the worldview of Newtonian-Cartesian Classical Physics have crumbled. These have been replaced by Uncertainties and probabilities of Quantum mechanics. *Perhaps the greatest revolution in the worldview of the new Physics has been engendered by the recognition that there is no purely objective observation.* The observing consciousness cannot be left out of the act of observation. Hisenberg's Uncertainty Principle tells us that each act of observation changes and distorts the system being so observed. Objectivity is a myth and it is time to recognise the fact that the consciousness of the observer is an inextricable part of the process of observation. This truth, the science of "Brahma Vidya", enunciated by the Atharvans, had realised almost 5000 years ago. It had gone much further. Consciousness is synonymous with Brahman. It is the ultimate ground state of this universe. My own teacher—the late Swami Pranvananda had simplified it like this: —

*"Everything in the Universe"*, he said *"is conscious.. The distinction between organic and inorganic, between the living and non-living is illusory.* Everything in this universe is conscious. *There is no "Jada" (inert) and "Chetan" (conscious). Everything, everywhere is a manifestation of that primal; substance—of consciousness".* The consciousness of the atom is absorbed in its whirling, the consciousness of the stones and rocks and minerals appears frozen and stratified; the consciousness of the trees and plants is rooted and immobile. It is however, the self same consciousness, expressed more actively in the fish and amphibians; in the reptiles and mammals and primates and also in man and in all trans-human entities that may exist anywhere else in this universe. Herein are the roots of a Universalist Religion—a religion that worships the ground state of the cosmos—

that reveres all forms of consciousness. Brahman is just another name for that existentialist infinity of aliveness, awareness and bliss.

**Ecology:** is the science of tomorrow. It deals with *the networks of supportive and symbiotic relationships that sustain the vibrant web of life and consciousness.* We learn from the Gaia theories that *the planet earth itself is a living organism* that is self-sustaining and self-organising. *Self-organising powers are the key manifestations of consciousness.* Ecology comes from the Greek word "Okios" (household). It is a study of the Earth household. This term was coined in the year 1865 by the German biologist Ernst Hackel who defined it as the science of relations between the organism and the surrounding world. In essence, ecology is all about networks and communities and symbiotic relationships that sustain growth and harmony. But what one is talking of here goes much deeper. One is referring to the concept of Depth Ecology. Erne Naess, a Norwegian philosopher had founded a school of philosophy in early 1970s called "Deep Ecology". Naess differentiated between "deep" and shallow concepts of Ecology.

**Shallow Ecology:** is Anthropocentric or "human-centred". It views humans as above and outside nature, as the source of all value and ascribe only instrumental or "use" value to Nature.

**Deep Ecology:** (As Fritjof Capra explains in his new magnum opus "The web of Life") does not separate humans or anything else from the natural environment. It does not see the world as a collection of isolated objects but as network phenomenon that are fundamentally inter-connected and inter-dependent. Deep Ecology recognises the intrinsic value of all living beings and views humans as just one particular strand in a web of life. Ultimately *deep ecological awareness is a spiritual or a religious aware-*

*ness*. When the concept of the human spirit is understood as *the mode of consciousness in which the individual feels a sense of belonging, of connectedness to the cosmos as a whole". Deep Ecology therefore is premised upon an intuitive understanding of a deeper connectivity of all life forms and* their arrangements in hierarchies of networks that support and sustain each other in relationships that are deeply symbiotic and nurturing.

## Madhu Vidya: The Wisdom of Honey

5000 years ago, the 'Atharvans' and the 'Angiras' sages who composed the Atharva Veda had come to startlingly similar conclusions. There is a very profound dialogue in the Atharva Veda between the Sage Dadhangya and the Ashwins—the twin Gods of the Vedic Pantheon. This is called the essence of the Madhu Vidya—or *the wisdom of Honey (Sweetness)*. Very simply put—it states—*"All things on this earth are honey (beneficial) to one another and to this earth. The earth in turn is honey (beneficial) to its creatures"*. This is the essence of ecology. When we talk of Brahma Vidya—we talk of the Depth Ecology—of the deeper basis of this ecological outlook. This outlook springs from the bedrock concept of consciousness. All things in this universe are conscious—only the degree and form of its manifestation varies. Underlying the bewildering and myriad diversity of forms and things in the universe lays the great unity of consciousness—of Brahman itself. Knowledge of that ground state of the universe—is the highest of all science. It is the Royal Science having known which all else is known.

*Deep Ecology today, is the basis for a new Universalist religion beyond narrow creeds*. A religion that was first spoken of in the mystic texts of the Atharva Veda, the mystic book of the Atharvans and Angira sages of the deep Indian Forests. It was recounted again in the Brihad Aranyaka Upanishads and the other sacred books of the Forest. It manifested again in the Ahimsa creed of reverence for all life forms that permeates the Indian religions of Buddhism and Jainism. The Universality of consciousness is the basis of the knowledge of Brahman. It is the central credo of mysticism.

*What mankind is heading for is a Paradigm shift in its basic outlook. It is evolving to a deeper spiritual outlook that recognises the universality of all consciousness everywhere in the cosmos.* Consciousness is the primal stuff out of which the cosmos is fashioned. That is the basic Paradigm of the new Science of Brahman.

*      *      *

"Trust the Force Luke"

Thus the mentor of Luke Skywalker exhorts the Jedi Knight in that very spiritual vision of the future contained in Science-Fiction Films of the "Star-Wars" genre. We could easily replace the word "Force" with the word "Field". "Trust the Field Luke"—the all-encompassing Morphogenetic Field of consciousness and Life itself; it gives rise to all living forms. The universal acceptance of the field view of life will cause a dramatic reversal of our basic scientific and social paradigms. *The Field view of life—as a vast Morphogenetic or Informational Energy field that encompasses everything in the universe, is likely to be the corner stone of our future religious beliefs.* It is a super intelligent field—it pervades every nook and cranny of the universe. It guides in its sweep, the dizzy motions of the giant galaxies, the pulsars and Quasars blink with its power—the quarks and charmed particles bob and dance and vanish on its surface like fleeting bubbles in an ocean of thoughts. It is the "One" that has become the "many". It is vast and grand and infinite and yet it is infinitesimally small. This cosmic field has a strange hologramic relationship with every individual entity that exists within its cosmic sweep. *Each particle of a hologram contains the entire picture.* Each individual manifestations of the field contains within itself (in a strange paradoxical fashion), the whole field. The field is not an amorphous sweep of impersonality, an entity less ocean with no waves of individuality. It is an infinity of intelligence, autonomous, self-existing and yet an inextricable part of the hologramic wholeness. *The field is a vast web of cosmic connectivity. Every part is linked with every other portion of the field in a bewildering phantasmagoria of symbiotic connections. Information spreads throughout its sweep in an instantaneous fashion, unencumbered by any cosmic speed limits of light or the inverse square laws of conventional physics.* The field is consciousness itself, multi-dimensional, luminescent, the source of all fusion and synthesis, holistic, hologramic, and indestructible, without beginning and without an end.

We are supposed to surrender our conscious sensors and faculties to the cascade-like descent of this force or the field.

"Trust the Force Luke" the words of the star warrior seem to give a prophetic vision of the future when the whole of mankind will worship not an anthropomorphic God or any cruel prophets of hate and intolerance but the universal goodness of the cosmic field. "Trust the Field". It is the fountainhead of all goodness, beauty and bliss. Let us be instruments for the expression of its super intelligence. Let us open ourselves to its goodness. Let us surrender ourselves to its infinite care. Let it guide our growth and destinies. Let it awaken us to the remarkable probabilities inbuilt into our future. For species evolution is not just pushed by the past; it is more imperiously pulled by the actualising thrust of the future. A thrust that seeks to actualise the waves of probabilities that cascade about in the cosmic field. Let us pray for a race of super creative, Brahmanical "Jedi'" twice born beings who have made themselves worthy instruments of the fields action. The wisdom of the field descends through them. They help to actualise its infinite possibilities. They help to express its brilliance and boundless super intelligence. They do not choose to serve the Field, the Field chooses them as its instruments. The Rig Vedic verse said: —

*"Jo Jaga Tam Richa Kamayante". The divine Richas (creative insights and inspirations, the archetypal concepts) are continually seeking the awakened minds. It is through their agency that they will be born. Through these illumined minds, the archetypal concepts will descend from the field.* Great complexity coexists with great simplicity. Some ten thousand years ago, when the earth was still young and homo-sapiens was struggling to move from the stage of the hunter-gatherer, the stone age nomad to a more settled form of agricultural life, the ancient Shamans had appeared on the scene. They manifested the first human urges for transcendence. The human brain is hard wired for religious/mystical experience. These simple, early humans looked upon the forces of nature with great awe and reverence. They worshipped the greats Blue sky as a god. They worshipped the spirits of the mountains and rivers and rocks and trees. The Shamans retired into solitude, to experience the depths of their own consciousness. They sang their simple songs; they beat their drums and danced. *They encountered ecstasy.* Shamanism was the world's first and most archaic technique of experiencing ecstasy. The ecstasy of Soma is what the Vedic seers also experienced in the great solitude. From the hatred and divisions of sects and creeds, let us return to that ecstatic and joyful simplicity of the Shaman and the seers of Soma. Today Scientists have conducted experiments using SPECT scans to establish the Neurobiological basis of mystical and religious experience. The human brain is hardwired for such experiences. The "God" circuits are in built in our biological organism. These are simply taken over by the

our biological organism. These are simply taken over by the ideological context of the World Religions. Our Gods' circuits impel
us to become believers. Religion has a deeply ingrained neuro-
biological basis. Today science has matured enough to study the
Neuro-theology of Nirvana. Let us experience the pure consciousness in ourselves. Let us realise its sameness everywhere. In the
sky, in the sea, in the mountains, in rivers and forests, in the steppes
and the deserts; in all creatures large and small, in all living things.
When we experience that unity we will experience ecstasy. With
ecstasy we will become Jedis—prophetic beings. The Kala Agni
will rise in us and cause the streams of Soma to descend. We will
be joyful and ecstatic once more. Soma will give us the gift of
incredible sweetness. We will learn compassion and give up hate
and discord. We will worship that great and infinite Field whose
love irrigates the cosmos. We will realise that the relationships in
nature are structured upon the underlying harmony of pure consciousness. The self-same consciousness exists in the minerals
and plants and trees, in the birds and bees, in the reptiles that
crawl and the mammals that walk and prowl the forests; in the
primates and homo-sapiens that stand erect and in many other
form of life on different star systems that orbit distant Suns.

"Trust the Field! Luke".

That benign and compassionate Field that nurtures and protects
all life forms will guide us—not just at the critical and stressful
junctures of our lives but also at every moment of our existence.
We must learn to trust, to let go, of our petty ego and separateness
from the cosmos. We must learn to meditate upon the universality
of our consciousness. When we touch it within we would have
touched the consciousness of all life forms everywhere in this vast
and expanding universe. We would have touched infinity and gained
the gift of ecstasy and joyfulness. We would look up at the hard

brilliance of the stars in the sky and feel the presence of entities and life form we cannot see. "Trust the Field", that vision of the starry eyed future of humanity may well graduate from science fiction to reality. Therein lies hope for our collective future.

The Gayatri hymn is the most sacred verse of the Vedas. It says, "We meditate upon *the brilliance of that resplendent Sun. May that sun shine upon our intelligence and illumine it for the good of all living beings*".

Another verse expostulates "Jyotisham Jyoti" "That light: That light of all lights". Visions of that light lead to experiences of Ecstasy, to the experience of Soma. *The Vedic metaphor of Honey— the essence of all sweetness, is the most apt metaphor for that experience of ecstasy, which imparts a deep Ecological experience of the cosmic connectivity of consciousness everywhere in this vast and expanding universe.*

# BIBLIOGRAPHY

## Books

1. Ann Arbor *"Spell Binders: Charismatic Political leadership"* West View Press New York 1985.

2. Arnold Magda B *"Emotions (Loyola Symposium on Feelings and Emotions)"* Ed. Arnold Magda. Loyola University Press 1960.

3. Arthur Avalon *"The Serpent Power"* Ganesh Publishers, Madras 1985

4. Ibid, *"The World as Power"* Ganesh Publishers, Madras 1986.

5. Sri Aurobindo *"The Life Divine"*. Sri Aurobindo Ashram press, Pondichery 1968/1965.

6. Ibid, *"Integral Yoga"* Sri Aurobindo Ashram Press Pondichery.

7. Ibid, *"The Secret of the Veda"*. Sri Aurobindo Ashram Press Pondichery, 1956.

8. Barbara Ann Brennan, *"Light Emerging: The Journey of Personal Healing"*, Bantam Books. New York, 1993.

9.  Bhom David, *"Wholeness and the Implicate Order"* New York. Harper and Row    1970.

10. Berner E (ed) (1971), *"R. Gordon Wasson on Soma and Daniel H.H. InglasResponse"*. Essay No 7 New Haven American Oriental Society.

11. Boyce.M. (1975), *"A History of Zorastrarianism"* Liden. E.J. Brill.

12. Capra Fritzof C, *"The Tao of Physics"* Shambala, Boston 1975, third updated edition 1991.

13. Ibid *"The Turning Point"* Shuman & Schuster, New York 1982.

14. Ibid *"Uncommon Wisdom"* Shuman & Schuster, New York 1985.

15. Ibid *"The Web of Life"* Flamingo, New York 1997.

16. Dr Choudhury Sujit K., *"Concise Medical Physiology"* New Central Books Agency. Calcutta (2nd Ed) 1993.

17. Colbrook H.T., *"On the Vedas or the Sacred Writings of the Hindus"*. Asiatic Researches (1805).

18. Griffith. R.T.H. Tram. *"The Hymns of the Rig Veda"* 2nd Ed. Delhi Motilal Banarasidas (1986).

19. Thomas S Kuhn. *"The Structure of Scientific Revolutions"* University of Chicago Press, Chicago (1970).

20. Marx Karl, *"Economic and Philosophical Manuscripts"* in Robert C Tucker Ed. The Marx -Engels Reader, New York, Norton (1972).

21. Gary Zukov, *"The Dancing Wu Li Masters"* Rider 1982.

22. R Gordon Wasson. *"Soma: The Divine Mushroom"* Harcourt, New York 1968.

23. Arthur Koestler, *"The Act of Creation"* Jonathan Cape, London 1952.

24. Ibid *"The Ghost in the Machine"* Rider, London 1956.

25. Ibid *"The Yogi and the Commissar"* Rider London 1962.

26. Castaneda Carlos *"The Teachings of Don Juan"* New York, Ballantyne 1968.

27. Ibid *"A Separate Reality"* New York, Ballantyne 1969.

28. Ibid, *"Journeys to Ixtilon"* Bantam Books New York, 1970.

29. Hisenberg, Werner, *"Physics and Philosophy"* New York, Harper and Row (1962).

30. Jung Carl Gustav, *"The Collected Works of Carl G. Jung"* Princeton, Princeton University Press (1928).

31. J. Krishnamurthy, *"Freedom from the Known"* New York, Harper and Row.

32. Marcia Eliade, *"Shamanism: Archaic Techniques of Ecstasy"*, Arkana Penguin, Saks London (1964).

33. Nyberg H, *"The Problem of the Aryans and Soma: The Botanical Evidence"*, In Erdosy (1995).

34. O'Flaherty W D, *"The Post Vedic History of the Soma Plant"*, In Soma Divine Mushroom of immortality Ed. R.G. Wasson, New York. Harcourt (1968).

35. Schumacher E F, *"Small is Beautiful"* New York: Harper and Row 1975.

36. A. Rupert Sheldrake, *"A New Science of Life: The Hypothesis of Formative Causation"* Bland and Brigs Ltd, London 1981.

37. Gopi Krishna *"The Kundalini"* Taraporevalla, Bombay, 1984.

38. Ibid, *"The Kundalini: The Biological Basis of Religion and Genius"* Taraporevalla, Bombay 1985.

39. E W Maoin in *"Altered States of Consciousness"* Ed by Charles T. Tart, John. Wiley and Sons.

40. Russell Trag and Jane Katra *"Miracles of Mind: Exploring Non-Local Consciousness"* New World Library, 1999.

41. Dr. James Austin, *"Zen and the Brain"*, Massachusetts Institute of Technology Press 1996

42. Alvin Toffler, *"Future Shock"*, Random House, New York, July 1970.

43. Ibid, *"The Third Wave"*, Bantam Books, New York.

## Articles and Papers

44. Dr Victor Benedict Arul "*A New Paradigm for the Reunification of Science*" Paper   quoted in Times of India 27 May 1986.

45. Issac Bentov "*Stalking the Wild Pendulum*" Paper in Lee Sanella's Book "*Kundalini: Psychosis or Transcendence*".

46. Wallace R.K. "*Physiological Effects of Transcendental Meditation*" Science Vol 1-67, (pp 1751-1754), 27 Mar 1970.

47. Karmatsu and Harai "*EEG Investigations of Zen Meditation*" Paper (1966) quoted in  Lee Sanella's, "*Kundalini: Psychosis or Transcendence*".

48. Stanley Jones, "*The Thermostatic Theory of the Biological Origin of Emotions*". Paper in Loyola Symposium on Emotions. Ed Magda B. Arnold. 1960.

49. Lee Sanella. "*Kundalini and Physio-Kundalini*" Paper in Journal of Philosophy. Indian Council of Philosophical Research Library, Lucknow.

50. H E Puthoff and R Trag, "*A Perceptual Channel for Information Transfer over Kilometre Distances: Historical Perspective and Recent Research*". Proc. IEEE, Vol 64 (1976) pp 329-354.

51. R Trag and HE Puthoff "*Information Transfer under Condition of Sensory Shielding*", Nature Vol 252 (1974). pp 602-607.

52. Vince Rouse "*Searching for the Divine*", Los Angles Time Magazine (Reproduced   in Readers Digest. Jan 02 Issue pp 125).

# OTHER TITLES ON INDIAN PHILOSOPHY FROM PILGRIMS PUBLISHING

- Inspirations from Ancient Wisdom (Anthology) ........ *Pilgrims Publishing*

- Krishnamurti: Two Birds on One Tree ..................... *Ravi Ravindra*

- Perfume of the Desert ................................. *Andrew Harvey and Eryk Hanut*

- The Atman Project ........................................................ *Ken Wilber*

- Up From Eden ........................................................ *Ken Wilber*

- Krishnamurti's Insight ....................................... *Hillary Rodrigues*

- The Light of Krishnamurti ............................... *Gabriele Blackburn*

- As the River joins the Ocean ........................... *G Narayan*

- Modern Hinduism ........................................... *W J Wilkins*

- The Foundations of Hinduism ............................ *Jadunath Sinha*

- Philosophy of Hindu Sadhana ........................ *Nalini Kanta Brahma*

- The Doctrine of Buddha ............................... *George Grimm*

- Buddhism: Its Essence and Development ............... *Edward Conze*

- The Song of the Atharvans ........................... *Brigadier G D Bakshi,*

www.pilgrimsbooks.com

*For Catalog and more Information Mail or Fax to:*

## PILGRIMS BOOK HOUSE

Mail Order, P. O. Box 3872, Kathmandu, Nepal
Tel: 977-1-4700919   Fax: 977-1-4700943
E-mail: mailorder@pilgrims.wlink.com.np